Daniel Connors

Celebrating The Fifty Days of Easter

XXIII
TWENTY-THIRD PUBLICATIONS
Mystic, Connecticut

To Deborah and Michael Patrick
who touch me daily with Easter fire

Twenty-Third Publications
P.O. Box 180
185 Willow Street
Mystic, CT 06355
(203) 536-2611

ISBN 0-89622-463-5
Library of Congress Catalog Card No. 90-71559

From Reviews of *Celebrating the Fifty Days of Easter*

"Connors's view of Easter as a season instead of just one Sunday is important liturgically and helpful to all Christians. He doesn't just say keep on celebrating Easter. He offers the reader a daily plan for keeping the Easter season alive in one's heart."

Peggy Weber
Catholic Observer

"A clearly and carefully presented reflection on the spirituality of the greatest season in the church's lectionary, *Celebrating the Fifty Days of Easter* will be very helpful to neophytes and life-long faithful. It is simple, direct, honest, and a valuable *vademecum* for the Christian pilgrim who takes the church year to heart."

James Lopresti
Former Executive Director
The North American Forum on the Catechumenate

"Connors has a rare gift: He speaks of our prayer, ritual, and tradition in a language most folks can understand. He makes sense of things spiritual and leads us to understand the spirituality of things sensible. Unless you opt to buy a copy for each parishioner, be sure that at least one copy makes it to your library for the spiritual enrichment of those who shape the prayer and ritual of your community's paschaltide."

Austin Fleming
Liturgy 90

"Here, at last, is a book that brings home the joy of the church's fifty days of Easter rejoicing! Homilists and all who prepare liturgy will find much food for thought, and recently married couples and new parents will relate especially well to the poignant stories capably told by one who shares the unique experiences of this time of life."

Paul Covino
Liturgical Resource Consultant

"*Celebrating the Fifty Days of Easter* is solid food for those newly enrolled in the faith community as well as daily food for the long-time disciple who wants to keep the fifty days of Easter alive at home, at work, or in school."

Rev. Jack Gilbert
Pastor, St. Mary Parish,
Marystown, Minnesota

"This book is designed to help both parishes and individuals fully experience and celebrate the real Easter for the fifty-day season from Easter Sunday to Pentecost—an early church custom being renewed...and this book tells us how to do it."

Ivan McIsaac
The New Freeman

"A recommendable resource for the neophyte....Though not explicitly stated I sense an underlying assumption in this author's work: we are called to be sacrament for the world. How right to have something designed for personal reflection be so mission-oriented. The best thing about all of this is that the author has created what can be a very fertile ground for reflection without violating or manipulating the Sunday lectionary. Isn't it amazing what can be created when we understand the church's liturgy and allow the lectionary to guide us in unfolding the mysteries we celebrate!"

Rev. Ron Oakham
Forum
The North American Forum on the Catechumenate

"Parish clergy, RCIA teams, and DREs should welcome *Celebrating the Fifty Days of Easter*. This is a clear, concise, usable vehicle to help guide everyone in the parish through the Easter season."

Dr. Mary Margaret Swogger
DRE, St. Peter the Apostle Church
Birmingham, Alabama

Contents

Introduction

The restored rites of Christian initiation are bringing many gifts to our church. They are helping us remember the community dimension of our faith. They are helping us rediscover insights into baptism, confirmation, and eucharist, and make connections with them. They are helping us remember that there are essential questions still facing us, still challenging us, as they have challenged every generation that has come before: What do the passion, death, and resurrection of Jesus mean for me in my life? What does God want me to do? What does it mean to be part of this church? What does it mean to be a Christian today?

As we take our turn struggling with these questions, the RCIA is also helping us remember that Christianity is not primarily about memorizing dogma or taking classes, but about learning to live as Christ lived. The rites show all of us—even those of us who received baptism, confirmation, and first eucharist as infants and children—that living as Christ lived calls for an adult commitment, a commitment to a journey we take with other people, a journey that grows and takes shape over time as we face the joys, sorrows, tedium, and anxious moments of our lives, and a journey that can be revealed most clearly by connecting our lives to the feasts and seasons of our church's liturgical year.

The entire liturgical year tells the story of the journey, but especially the ninety days from Ash Wednesday to Pentecost Sunday. This is the season that, above all, reveals the paschal mystery, the saving death and resurrection of Christ and of our part in it. Lent is the church's great retreat, the church's spring training, as early church Fathers spoke of it. ("Lent" comes from an old Anglo-Saxon word for "spring.") It is the time of intense preparation for the Triduum, and especially for the sacraments of initiation to be celebrated at the Easter Vigil when the elect come to the font and the assembly renews and remembers its own journey to the water.

At this point, the renewed rites of initiation have given us yet another gift. They have restored to us a great treasure of our ancestors, a full fifty-day season of joy from Easter Sunday to Pentecost. Most of us didn't grow up thinking of Easter as being fifty days long. The trumpets volleyed on Easter Sunday, and then the church stayed fairly quiet until Pentecost. Now we are able to savor what our ancestors savored, a special time for delving into the mysteries we have celebrated, a season rich in Scripture and liturgical prayer, a season that can reveal so much about the Christian life.

This book was written to help you begin to get in touch with this Easter season by offering a reflection for each of the fifty days. It was written for newly baptized adults, for RCIA teams, for parents who are helping their children prepare for sacraments, and for all members of the church who are struggling with what it means to follow Christ.

On weekdays, the reflections concern the prayers of the Sunday liturgies of the Easter season and the Easter Scriptures for year A of the liturgical cycle, the year considered especially suitable to the RCIA (RCIA, 247). The Scripture citations are given so that you can look up and read the passage before turning to the reflection. On Sundays, always a special day of feasting, we'll look at the meaning of Easter and some of the special symbols of the season—baptism, gathering, water, oil, light, bread, and wine.

These reflections are not a catechism of Easter dogma. They are certainly not the final word on what Easter or the sacraments or Christian life is all about. They are the personal reflections of someone who, like you, struggles with what it means to be a disciple today, with what it means to be baptized, with what it means to belong to this church. These reflections came out of my own pilgrim journey, and I hope you will use them as a starting point for deepening your own encounter with the risen Christ. As individuals, as families, and as small groups, let these reflections mingle with the Easter stories of your own life, and share your stories with one another so that, over the Easters of a lifetime, the meanings and glory of the season may fill your lives.

Easter Sunday

The Meaning of Easter

The cathedral was packed that Easter morning. Even from a distance you could hear the people inside. "Glory to God!" they shouted. "God be praised!" they cried. But the noise they made then was nothing compared to what came when their bishop entered the church and advanced through their midst. Then everyone was standing and the sound of the assembly exploded into an almost deafening roar of joy. Their bishop, the great Augustine, reached his place in the assembly and waited. Finally the assembly grew quiet and he greeted them. It was all they needed. Like a thunderclap they burst again into spontaneous cries, and with arms outstretched and joy in their hearts, they praised the goodness of their God....

Don't expect this to happen in your parish church on Easter Sunday. Our Easter celebrations will be somewhat quieter and our joy a little more restrained than that of Augustine's fifth-century Christians. Part of that is surely owing to cultural differences, for we tend to be somewhat quieter and more restrained in church.

But aren't more than cultural differences at play here? Do we really feel the same joy they felt? Is there an Easter song building inside us that would just burst out if our sense of propriety didn't hold it back? Or did our ancestors in the faith find something in this celebration that we often seem to miss?

For them, Easter was filled with such profound joy that a single day was not nearly enough time to celebrate it. From as far back as at least the middle of the second century and for many centuries thereafter, they celebrated Easter as a fifty-day feast, lasting from the first Alleluias of the Vigil until evening prayer on the day of Pentecost.

Our ancestors found great meaning in this fifty-day period. Fifty days was a symbol of eternity. Fifty days is seven weeks—a week of weeks—plus one day. This was the eighth day, the same name they used for the day of resurrection, the same name they used for Sunday, the first day of the week. For them this eighth day was not just the start of a new seven-day week, but the beginning of a whole new creation, the beginning of life in the Spirit, the beginning of the last days, the celebration of life in Christ.

And there is more. Fifty days is about one-seventh of the year. They hold the same relation to the year as Sunday holds to the week.

These fifty days of Easter, therefore, were the "Great Sunday" of the year, one celebration, a time when kneeling and penance were forbidden and joyous songs of Alleluia filled the air. This was the time to bask in the glory of the risen Christ. This was the special time to rejoice with the *neophytes*, the new members of the community who had been initiated into the faith through baptism, confirmation, and eucharist at the Easter Vigil celebration that began the season. And for the neophytes, these fifty days were known as the time of *mystagogy*, the time to gather with their bishop and deepen their understanding of the mysteries they had experienced.

As it was for them, so it is again for us now. If we do not yet share their enthusiasm for the season, perhaps part of the difference lies in what we think we are celebrating. We decorate our churches with shrouds draped over crosses, and banners decorated with empty tombs and "He is risen" slogans. We either act as if we are commemorating something that happened only to Jesus almost 2000 years ago, or we sing "Jesus Christ Is Ris'n Today," and misunderstand it to mean that in some way the historical Jesus has once again climbed out of the tomb.

But Jesus rose only once and will never die again, and 2000 years is a long time to sustain excitement about a historical event, no matter how significant. Usually our celebrations need to be rooted a little closer to home. So what is Easter really all about?

Perhaps our fifth-century ancestors knew what so many of us must relearn and believe: Easter does not just celebrate something that happened to Jesus. Easter is a celebration of what happens to *us* because of Jesus. Easter celebrates how we have been baptized into Jesus' death and resurrection, and now share his mission through the work of his Spirit. Easter celebrates how Jesus dies and rises in *us* here and now, in this parish, in this place, in our jobs and families, in all our joys and sorrows in this world.

Easter is a time for us to bask in what the risen Christ is doing for us and in us. It is time to rejoice in the presence of the neophytes in our midst, for they are the sign that Christ continues to renew the church. It is a time to share our stories of dying and rising with one another, and to see more clearly how we, as individuals and as a church, are called to share in Christ's work.

Once we start to get a sense of what all this means, how could we possibly restrain our excitement, or our joy?

Toward the Second Sunday of Easter

Acts 2:42–47
Psalm 118:2–4,13–15,22–24
1 Peter 1:3–9
John 20:19–31

MONDAY

When I was little, I loved to put myself into Bible stories. When my father would read the Passion to us on Good Friday afternoon, I would see myself coming to Jesus' rescue. On Easter I would see myself in the garden with Mary or going to the empty tomb with Peter and the Beloved Disciple. How wonderful it would be to meet the risen Lord and then run to tell everyone what I had found out. If I had been there... how glorious, how exciting it would have been.

But I wasn't there, and that used to make me sad. I envied the disciples who could see and hear and touch Jesus, who could believe that he had conquered death because they had seen it for themselves.

This week's Scripture readings are aimed at all of us little children who grew up believing that it would have been wonderful to have been there, but whose adult faith has to be based on what the disciples *tell* us of Christ. We are the people in the first reading who rely on the teaching of the disciples. We, too, are the ones who are told in the second reading that "although you have never seen him you love him, and...believe in him, and rejoice...." And in the gospel, Jesus is thinking of us all when he says "Blessed are they who have not seen, but have believed."

The readings only begin there, however. They go on to show us just how fully we are blessed and how, through baptism, we enter a life where we too, right now, can meet and touch the risen Christ and share in his mission.

Let the readings and the prayers of the liturgy for the Second Sunday of Easter lead you into this new life. On Sunday, we will take a further look at baptism, which is where this new life begins.

TUESDAY

First Reading: Acts 2:42–47
"The brethren devoted themselves to the apostles' instruction and the communal life, to the breaking of bread and the prayers....Those who believed shared all things in common."

St. Paul spoke of Christ as the new Adam (Romans 5). In this Sunday's first reading, we hear a description of the new Adam's garden of Eden.

The author of Acts knew that this first Christian community would soon be torn by dissent, doubt, and human failings. His purpose in telling us about it was not to make us yearn for the good old days or feel guilty about parish life today, but to show the signs of the Spirit beginning to act through the body of Christ, the community, the church. This reading gives us a summary of what it means to be the body of Christ. Where we see these signs, we see Christ living and active in our world.

Where are these signs in our world today? Where do we see Christ moving? We see Christ in the Word, the "apostle's instructions" handed down to us. We see Christ when his body, the church, gathers for prayer and especially for eucharist. We see Christ reaching out into the world when the members of his church put the needs of other people first.

When families struggle to live in harmony and to accept the different strengths and weaknesses of each member, when they put the needs of others before their own needs, when parishes struggle to live in harmony and to respect the gifts of each member, when our concern and action for the poor move beyond special events and Christmas and happen every day, when we struggle to understand that being a eucharistic people means acting in and serving the world no matter what the cost—when signs like these happen, then we who have not seen but still believed are truly blessed, for we are living our mission, and we too look upon the face of Christ.

Where do you see Christ moving in your life? What signs of Christ do you see in your family? In your parish?

WEDNESDAY

Responsorial Psalm: Psalm 118:2–4,13–15,22–24
"The stone which the builders rejected has become the cornerstone…."

When we see how God is moving and active in our world, and what God has done for us, there is nothing more fitting than to sing a song of thanks and praise. Psalm 118 is such a song, and we join with the house of Israel, and the house of Aaron, and all who fear the Lord in proclaiming that God's love is everlasting and God's mercy endures forever.

Scripture scholars generally believe that the "I" in this song refers to the whole nation of Israel. Hard pressed by enemies, Israel found its strength and courage, help and victory in God. Little Israel, the stone rejected (i.e., of no account with the powerful nations), becomes the cornerstone, and it is the Lord who has done this wonderful thing.

Christian tradition, at least as far back as the gospels, has applied the verse about the cornerstone to Christ. He who was held of no account has proven to be the cornerstone of our new life in God.

Rescued in the waters of baptism, we need to cry out that God's mercy and love endure forever. We who are nourished in the sacraments, and supported by others in our family and community, should sing of the strength and courage that have come to us from the body of Christ.

And while we sing, we need to remember that through baptism we are all members of the body of Christ. In the thousands of small events of everyday life, we can also bring the mercy, love, strength, courage, and salvation of our God to others. We are all stones of little consequence built into the great cornerstone so that others may build upon us.

In what ways have you felt the mercy and love, strength and courage of our God? In what ways can you bring these gifts to others?

THURSDAY

Second Reading: 1 Peter 1:3–9
"He who in his great mercy gave us new birth."

While the first reading and the gospel focus on the Christian life of both recognizing and being the presence of Christ, the second reading speaks of the way we enter that life—the waters of baptism. Many scholars believe that the sections from First Peter that we read during the Sundays of Easter are in fact hymns taken from a very ancient baptismal liturgy.

Looking at the reading from this perspective can only increase its power for us. Imagine when this reading was first proclaimed. It was a time of persecution in the very young church, a time when just being a Christian was enough reason to be killed and the baptismal waters of life might just bring about your earthly death. But there, with the threat of terror and suffering all around, the church sang of new birth, hope, imperishable inheritance, inescapable joy touched with glory, and the trials, sufferings, and distress that would only serve to show how genuine was this baptismal act of faith.

Christians still suffer and die for their faith, but most of us seem to face milder forms of persecution these days. Perhaps we need to learn again, as our modern martyrs and the early Christians show us, that following Jesus really is about life and death, and self-giving unto death for a share in everlasting joy.

When we struggle to move our faith beyond social convention, we are likely to start finding out what following Jesus can really mean. When we treat others with forgiveness and justice, we can start to see how hard our faith is and what it can cost. Even deciding what is just or unjust and what action should be taken can lead to much distress. Every day we face these little trials that can bring us closer to the life Jesus lived.

How do you meet these trials in your own life? How do you participate in the dying and rising of Jesus, so that your newborn faith may be "genuine" and "more precious than the passing splendor of fire-tried gold"?

FRIDAY

Gospel: John 20:19–31
"These have been recorded to help you believe that Jesus is the Messiah."

A church filled with harmony and self-giving, a baptismal people facing persecution with expressions of great joy—behind it all is the risen Christ who appears in this gospel. John is careful to point out that only some of Jesus' signs have been recorded, and these for a set purpose: so that those of us who have not seen may believe.

If we are to believe in Christ, we must first know him. And we who did not see him must learn to meet him through his signs. Today's gospel reveals some of those signs: Jesus comes and stands with his disciples. He shows them his wounds, still visible and real on his risen body. He says "Peace be with you." He breathes the holy Spirit on them. He sends them out on a mission of reconciliation.

Here then are a few of the signs by which we can know Christ. We can find him in the Christian community, the gathering of his disciples. We can see him acting as his community carries out its mission and reaches out with the breath of the Spirit it received from him. But there is more. When people work for justice and reconciliation, there is Christ. When men and women sacrifice and offer themselves for others, there is Christ. When we see the scars that come from self-giving, there is Christ. When we see the poor and exploited, covered with the scars caused by the selfishness and power of others, there too is our Christ.

Our world is full of the signs of Christ. We need to find those signs so that we too may know him and share his mission—a mission proclaiming that death and resurrection are two sides of the same reality, a mission proclaiming in wondrous signs that giving our life for others is the only way to have life in his name.

How have you come to know Christ through his signs? In what ways are you a sign of Christ to others?

SATURDAY

The Liturgical Prayers

The prayers of the Mass of the Second Sunday of Easter focus on the gift of baptism. In the opening prayer we pray that God will renew the gift of life within us. In the prayer after communion we pray that the sacraments of Easter—baptism, confirmation, and eucharist—will live forever in our minds and hearts.

It's important to remember that when the priest says these prayers, he is praying on behalf of us all. Our "Amen" is our confirmation that this is our prayer, that we too are asking this of God through Christ our Lord.

To ask for a renewal of our baptism and that the initiation sacraments will live forever in our hearts, is to ask for something very wonderful and very fearful. It means that we want these gifts to be really present in our lives. It means that we must want to move beyond the pious talk stage and find ways to make them a reality every day.

For some of us that may mean spending time, alone or with others, looking for the presence of Christ in our world. It may mean pushing aside thoughts of deadlines and quotas to do nothing but celebrate the joy of that presence. It may mean spending more time with family and friends and speaking about what our faith means to us. It may mean searching for a deeper understanding of baptism. It may mean challenging ourselves and each other to take a risky step into the dying and rising life of our savior, perhaps by finally spending some time at the local soup kitchen, initiating a food collection as part of the parish offertory collection, supporting those who are on the front lines of justice, examining how we treat others in our work and at home, or digging more deeply into what our pope and bishops and the rest of our tradition say about justice and peace.

There are many ways to bring baptism to life in our lives. The crucified-risen Christ of the gospel beckons us. The community reaches out to support us. God stands ready to answer this prayer. Discovering and living the answer is up to us.

SECOND SUNDAY OF EASTER

Baptism

I met him, of all places, at a baptism class. We were both fathers preparing for the baptism of our children, but with one major difference between us. I was a "cradle Catholic" baptized as an infant, and he was a catechumen also preparing for his own baptism at the Easter Vigil.

As we talked I grew a little envious. Everything about baptism was new and filled with grace for him. For me, listening to him was very much like discovering the world anew through the eyes and descriptions of a child. As he described his own path to the font, the powers of light and darkness, the touch of water, the importance of this community all took on fresh meaning for me. A few months later I saw his face as he came up out of the water at the Vigil, and for the first time in my life I started to see what baptism is really all about.

Easter only makes sense when you are in touch with baptism. And that puts many of us who were baptized as infants at a disadvantage. We don't remember our own baptism, and when we think of baptism in general, it's usually in terms of what we were taught as children—that baptism washes away original sin and makes it possible for us to go to heaven. Baptism does indeed do these things, but sometimes these words can hide the richness of the sacrament from us.

When you were baptized, the power of Satan, the spirit of evil, was cast out of you. You were rescued from the kingdom of darkness so that you might live in God's light. Through baptism you were joined to the body, the community, the family of Christ, and you were called to share the fullness of life in that family. You received a share of the citizenship of the saints in heaven. Baptism means a total conversion of who you are—you entered the baptismal waters to die with Christ so that you might share in his passover from death to life. In your baptism you became part of Christ, you were empowered to live as he lived, and to slowly, over a lifetime, put to death all that is not Christ in you. In baptism you were called to die to self, to live for others, to accept that the risen Christ is also the crucified Christ, and to realize that you share in his resurrection only to the extent that you share in his mission. Through baptism you received the power to be Christ's arms and legs and voice for others. In your baptism, you became a sign to the world of the redeeming action of our God.

Such images are but a small part of the richness of baptism, a richness so often hidden, a richness so vast that even 2000 years of Christianity have not exhausted its meaning.

What meaning does such language have for you? "Do you reject Satan?...Do you believe in God?..." The first time you heard those questions you were probably too young to understand the words. Your godparents and parents held you close, and as you were washed in water and anointed with oil, they made promises to help you grow in faith. Now that you are an adult you are still on that faith journey, and as you stand amid the Christian community you are called to remember your baptism, to accept or reject this great gift of God, and to find the meaning of the words and images by living them out in the cycles and seasons of your life.

For a Christian, to *remember* something means to tap into its power. It means to act in such a way that what you recall lives again *in you*. For that reason, nothing is more important than remembering your baptism. If memories of your own are too distant to recall, remember the catechumens you saw baptized at the Easter Vigil. Remember the baptisms of your sons and daughters, nieces and nephews, grandsons and granddaughters. Remember the baptismal promises you renewed on Easter.

When you enter your church for Mass, the first thing you might do is to touch the water. As you touch it, remember baptism. As you bring that water to your forehead to make the sign of the cross, remember in whose name you were baptized. As you enter the worship space, look around at all your brothers and sisters who have also touched the water and who share the baptismal journey with you. As you come down the aisle, look up at the paschal candle and see the Christ whose body you have all become. Look at the burning flame and remember the light of resurrection that baptism promises. Then look at the red grains of incense marking the wounds of the crucified Christ, and remember the kind of life your baptism calls you to lead.

And as you listen to the Scripture readings, remember what they are—and what you are called to be—a testament, a witness, the voice of a people on fire with what it means to die and be reborn in Christ.

Toward the Third Sunday of Easter

Acts 2:14,22–28
Psalm 16:1–2,5,7–8,9–10,11
1 Peter 1:17–21
Luke 24:13–35

MONDAY

Our friend's nephew had just been born with heart disease and there didn't seem to be much hope. We promised to pray for him and we prayed every day. We prayed for little Daniel through all his operations. When our own son came successfully through heart surgery on Ash Wednesday, we rejoiced and thanked God and prayed that Daniel would also be saved.

But Daniel died during the Easter season, a few days before his six-month day, and we cried for him. I asked God why it had to happen. I held my own child and thought of Daniel's parents—what must they think of prayer and God?

They were exhausted and sad, but there was no despair, no accusations, no blame. Our friend wrote to us of how Daniel's entire family had received strength from the funeral liturgy, how so many of the words seemed to be aimed directly at them, and how, even in their grief, they found great joy in knowing their son was with God. Our friend wrote of the choir, and all the people of the parish who had come to help and be with them at this time. Everything in her letter spoke of God's presence and love. In a special way, Daniel's family was living one of the central messages of this week's Scripture readings: Believe that God always stays close to us, and transforms our sorrow into joy.

Believing in the risen Christ is not as easy as it sounds. Believing and celebrating seem easy when things are going well for us, but what happens when things go badly? Do we cast about for villains to blame for our troubles, like Peter and Cleopas do in the coming Sunday's readings? Do we think God only walks with us when things are going well? Do we see how central the death of Jesus is to our Easter joy? Do we see how our baptism calls us as much to death as to life?

Think of these questions as you read the Scripture this week. Through the readings, let God call you deeper into the paschal mystery, the dying and rising of Jesus. Let baptism be your entry into that mystery, and let the gathering of the community give you the strength to live and rejoice in it every day of your life.

TUESDAY

First Reading: Acts 2:14,22–28

"You even used pagans to crucify him and kill him, but God freed him from death's bitter pangs."

In this reading, Peter uses some very strong words, words that have helped to feed hatred and bigotry for centuries. The church now officially acknowledges that the harsh New Testament language against the Jews does not reflect the situation at the time of Jesus, but comes from a later period when the early church felt itself pulling away from Judaism. We now know that to blame the Jewish people for the death of Christ, as Peter seems to do here, is both inaccurate and unjust.

Perhaps we are all like Peter. When something goes wrong, our first impulse may be to run away from suffering (as Peter even denied knowing Jesus) and then look for someone else to blame. If all else fails, we blame our suffering on God. We say that it must be God's will.

But this reading calls us to a deeper understanding. It tells us, first, that God hates suffering, for through his "miracles, signs and wonders," Jesus spent his ministry fighting against suffering wherever he found it. The reading tells us that God stays very close to us when we suffer. It tells us that suffering is not God's will, but it has become part of God's *plan*. It tells us that through Jesus' self-giving, God has transformed suffering and given it meaning—Jesus suffered and died that we might live. Jesus' life of self-giving so strongly connected him to God's transforming love and justice that "it was impossible for death to hold him," and so God "raised him up again."

What do these words mean in our lives? Can we accept that suffering, death, and resurrection go hand in hand—for us as well as for Christ? When and how can we feel God close to us in suffering? Can we share God's anger when people suffer because others (like us?) refuse to accept even small discomforts? Do we think of how our baptism calls us to put others first? What more can we do, today, to relieve the suffering of others? And, like Peter, can the transforming joy of our Easter faith grow stronger than our human fear?

WEDNESDAY

Responsorial Psalm: Psalm 16:1–2,5,7–8,9–10,11
"You will show me the path to life, fullness of joys in your presence."

The first reading this week is a hard one to bear. It tells us that we cannot celebrate Easter without taking part in the defeat that leads to victory. It tells us that Christ did not come to give us a reward for keeping the rules of a middle-class lifestyle or to save us from the pain and suffering that is a natural part of life. It tells us, instead, that Christ lived and died that life itself might be redeemed, and that we might find meaning and redemption in the midst of life's ordinary joys and pain. It tells us that suffering is not the ultimate evil; the ultimate evil is living only for oneself.

No normal person likes pain. We all hope and pray that we will be spared suffering. But that is not the promise of Easter. And knowing that can make us afraid: Who among us has the courage to live what Easter is really about?

When we are frightened, we often sing a song to bolster our courage, to lift our spirits, to fill us with strength. The church invites us to respond to the first reading with such a song, and to sing of our God who walks with us, who offers us refuge and counsel, who holds fast our lot.

In singing this song we can't pretend that God will save us

from the pain of being human. The Jewish people were singing this song for at least 500 years before Peter made it the song of Jesus, and their story can hardly be seen as moving from triumph to triumph. The same is true of us. For Christians, it is Jesus who "shows us the path of life," and that path leads in one direction: up a hill to a cross.

But we sing with glad hearts, and our souls rejoice, because God will never abandon us on our path. God's love will ultimately transform our nights into days, and we will share the fullness of joys in God's presence forever.

Have you ever felt abandoned or lost? How has God given you refuge and hope? What or who brought God's comfort to you?

THURSDAY

Second Reading: 1 Peter 1:17–21

"You were delivered from your futile way of life...by Christ's blood beyond all price."

In this reading, we again hear the early church speaking to its newly initiated members. These are also the words that we need to speak to the newly baptized members of our own parishes. They are words that must constantly stay fresh in our hearts as well.

Their message is this: Baptism is an event that changes everything about us. It changes everything so much that we seem like travelers in a strange land. It calls us to see differently into matters of life and death, suffering and sacrifice. It calls us to move beyond a "futile way of life" and go deeper into a plan of God that has been unfolding since the creation of the world. At the center of this plan is Christ, who by his dying and rising has redeemed and saved us. Through him we come to God.

The reading does not call us to change. It tells us that we are already changed. We are already living in the "last days." The time to prepare for baptism is over. Now is the time to keep our faith and our hope centered on God and to live like the baptized people we already are.

How do we live as baptized people? The Easter seasons of a lifetime will help us discover the answer. And each person's answer will be different. But each answer will be centered on Christ, the unblemished lamb who gave willingly, who died that others might live.

When has your faith led you to feel like a traveler in a strange land? In what ways does your faith call you to see things differently than the vision of life usually presented in our popular culture? In what ways do you see your actions following in the path of Christ? Where do you find the life of Christ most active today? What is God asking of you today?

FRIDAY

Gospel: Luke 24:13–35
"They had come to know him in the breaking of the bread."

Living a baptismal commitment, believing that the plan of God transforms and gives meaning to sacrifice and suffering, knowing that God calls us to follow Christ into a death that leads to glory—the first and second readings this week may leave us feeling like Cleopas and his unnamed companion. Like them, we can be very slow to understand the ways of God. Like them, we may succumb to confusion and despair. Like them, when trouble comes, we may be ready to run out on our baptismal commitment and leave the community back in Jerusalem.

But God does not abandon us. God comes after us. God walks with us even when we don't recognize it. God is always inviting us, always ready to transform our weakness and bring us strength. For Cleopas and his companion this invitation came in an encounter with a stranger. For us, it comes every Sunday in the eucharistic liturgy. The two invitations are very much the same.

The stranger invites the two disciples to tell him what they are talking about. They tell him of their struggles and their discouragement. The stranger reveals God's plan and Christ's presence in the Scriptures, and although they do not yet understand, their hearts burn within them. They invite the stranger to eat with them, and at the meal he becomes the host, breaking bread and giving it to them. In that moment, that moment of breaking and giving, the dying and rising Christ is plain to them, and as he vanishes from their sight they rise and return with renewed strength to the Jerusalem community and their baptismal life.

Liturgy of the word, liturgy of the eucharist—for the two disciples on the way to Emmaus, and for us, this is one of the most powerful ways that God speaks to us and strengthens us. It is the way we rededicate ourselves to our baptism and enter more deeply into our mission of dying and rising. The eucharist strengthens us for our struggles with life's discouragement and pain. And it begins and ends in charity and hospitality, for in our openness to strangers and in the gathering of a caring, giving community, we see the face of Christ.

SATURDAY

The Liturgical Prayers

In general, we Catholics are much more comfortable celebrating Lent than we are celebrating Easter. If we apply a lenten perspective to the Scripture we have prayed over and reflected on this week, our natural reaction may be to see how inadequate we are, how far we fall from fulfilling our baptismal commitment, how slow we are to respond to Christ's invitation to follow him into the paschal mystery, the dying and rising that brings redemption. We can feel guilty that our humdrum lives seem to fall so short of what God asks of us.

But during these fifty days we must constantly remind ourselves that Easter is not Lent. This is not a time for guilt. This is a time to rejoice because Christ has conquered death and brought us salvation. This is the time to celebrate the transformation God has already begun in us, a transformation God has promised to bring to completion. This is a time to get in touch with the grace of God present and victorious in our world and to face the challenge of helping the world come to see the kingdom of God in its midst.

The opening prayers, the prayer over the gifts, and the prayer after communion for the Third Sunday of Easter stress this Easter perspective. In them we acknowledge that God has already made us sons and daughters. We say that we are already newborn people. We testify that God has already given us great joy. We also pray that we may continue to look forward with hope, that we may be strengthened, and that God will bring us to perfection and into glory.

You could do nothing more valuable today than to think about how God is already at work in your life. Think of the times you have sacrificed for others. Think, for example, of how often you've put up with monotony on the job or arrogant bosses for the sake of your family. Think of how others have sacrificed or gone even a small distance out of their way to make something better for you. Think of the love you have given and received in your life. Think of the kindness you have given to or received from strangers. Think of how suffering has changed you or brought you closer to others. Think of the beauty of the world God has given us.

Look around at all the ways you are working in God's plan, and pray that what has already begun may be fulfilled.

THIRD SUNDAY OF EASTER

Gathering

Before there was Lent, there was Easter, and before there was Easter, there was Sunday.

For the early Christians, Sunday was the first day of the week. It was also called the eighth day, because it didn't just start a new week—it was the beginning of a new way of life, a new creation. Sunday was also the day of the resurrection, the day of light, the day of the Spirit. And from the beginning, Sunday was the special day of the *gathering*.

We use many signs and symbols and images (some weak, some strong) to speak of Easter in our churches—empty tombs, empty shrouds draped over crosses, spring flowers, flowing water. But the greatest Easter symbol of all, greater even than the paschal candle or the baptismal font, is the Sunday gathering of the assembly of believers.

From the earliest days in the upper room, we Christians have *gathered* on Sunday to tell the story of Jesus, to recognize the risen Lord in the Scriptures and in the "breaking of the bread," to initiate new members into the gathering, and to strengthen the gathering through the practice of reconciliation. In this way we celebrate the paschal mystery, the mystery of how, by dying, Jesus destroyed our death and, by rising, restored our life, how he lives today in us, the gathering of his followers, still really present, saving and redeeming, and how he will come again in glory at the end of time.

To be part of the gathering is to be part of this mystery. When you are alone, you are a disciple of Jesus. When you gather, you become the body of Christ. You become God's active presence.

You become Christ's sacrament to the world, because through you, the world feels the power of the risen Christ moving in its midst.

No one comes to the risen Christ alone. It is often said, sometimes snidely, that young people come back to the church after they have children. But rather than see that as an indictment of young people, isn't it a testament to how much we need others in our pilgrimage to Christ? My son Michael needs me to help him grow in Christ. At the same time I need *him*. He is a focus, a prod for my own life on the journey; in nurturing him I, too, am nourished. We bring one another to God.

And as it is between parent and child, so it is between members of the community. Christ invites us, the broken, the lame, the selfish, the confident, the rich and the poor, friends and strangers, newly baptized adults, and cradle Catholics. Christ invites us all to gather as a community of forgiven sinners, to be united in him, to share his body, and be strength and nourishment for one another.

But that is not the end of the mystery. Christ invites us deeper into the gathering, to a purpose *beyond* ourselves. An assembly concerned only with itself ends up singing jolly songs and wishing one another a nice day. But we are called to be the body of Christ, and that means being like Christ. It means being a community that lives for *others*.

We often tend to act as if liturgy and the world have little to do with one another, as if Mass is an oasis from the world. I recently heard a priest tell the people that "When you come to Mass you should be thinking of nothing but the Mass. You shouldn't be thinking about your job, or your kids, or anything else *but* the Mass." But I don't think Mass makes any sense if you can't connect it with your job and your kids, and all the other concerns that fill your day. We live in this world, and Christ was born in this world, and Christ calls us to gather in him so that we might join him in gathering and redeeming *this* world.

So when you gather for Mass, bring the world with you. Bring Uncle Joe's alcoholism, and that report you can't finish on time. Bring your worries about your teenager's behavior, and your desire for that new sportscar. Bring the memory of the homeless and hungry people you have seen, and the violence on last night's news. Bring the patient you thought was getting better who died when you didn't expect it. Yes, even bring that funny sound that just started to show up in the plumbing.

Bring them all to Christ. Gather with your brothers and sisters who have brought their own concerns, and let Christ gather up your lives in an offering to the Father. And God will respond, but not with instant solutions or mini-lessons of personal advice. God doesn't respond by telling you what to *do*. God responds by showing you what you are to *become*. In the gathering, God's Spirit responds by revealing the Christ. Listen as a community to Christ revealed in Scripture. Let that revelation lead you to the gathering at his banquet, so that you may be nourished with his body broken and blood poured out, so that you may return to the world to be body broken and blood poured out for others.

For when you gather for Mass, God invites you to act out in ritual what you are called to do every day of your life—to share in Christ's paschal mystery—to die to self so as to live for others, to gather and share with strangers, to reconcile, to nourish, to work for justice, to praise and proclaim God's overwhelming love and mercy in the face of every human terror, and to continue doing this, Sunday after Sunday, season after season, year after year until all the words and actions take root in you—so that you and the world and all the members of Christ's body, past, present, and future, may one day live forever in that eighth day and join St. Paul in saying, "I live now, not I, but Christ lives in me."

This is the mystery your baptism calls you to. This is what gathering is for. This is what Easter is all about.

Toward the Fourth Sunday of Easter

Acts 2:14,36–41
Psalm 23:1–3,3–4,5,6
1 Peter 2:20–25
John 10:1–10

MONDAY

Russell lived three houses away. He was eight and I was five. We would play cowboys or soldiers and have adventures in the undeveloped fields behind our street. He was my hero and I would follow him anywhere.

One day we were crawling along the ground with our tommy guns when Russell suddenly stopped and pointed to a small wasp that was disappearing under the grass. "That's a 'swamp wasp,'" he said. "They live here in the ground and they hate kids. If you bother them they'll follow you and sting you 'til you die."

I realize now that he was testing me. Back then I trusted him, and I was afraid. "Don't go near it," I said. But he stood up and stepped toward it. "If they come out," he said, "run for those bushes." "Russ! Don't!" I pleaded. But he did. He stomped on the spot where the wasp had disappeared and yelled "run!" He sped past me toward the small thicket and I ran after him, sure that a swarm of angry wasps had come out of the ground straight for me. I didn't want to die. I ran as fast as I could, and I jumped into the thicket, crying and trembling and wheezing with fear.

"They won't come in here," he said. "But they'll wait for you and they'll get you when you come out." I clutched my toy gun and whimpered. "What are we going to do?" A smile started to spread across his face. "I don't know," he said. "But the wasps didn't see me. By the time they got out of the ground all they saw was you. They aren't after *me. I* can leave whenever I want." And with that my hero and leader got up, left the bushes, and ran to his house. I crouched in those bushes and cried after him. I pleaded with him to tell me what to do. But he was gone, and I hid there all afternoon and cried, until my father came out looking for me and brought me home.

All of us have had our experience with false shepherds—persons or things we've put our trust in only to end up feeling betrayed, abandoned, and trapped. That's why we should take special delight during Easter in celebrating Jesus Christ, the true shepherd. As you pray over the Scripture this week, think about the false shepherds you have known, and how Christ, through the waters of baptism, leads you through the only door that leads to life.

TUESDAY

First Reading: Acts 2:14,36–41
"You must reform and be baptized in the name of Jesus Christ."

Last week we heard the beginning of Peter's first proclamation of the good news. This week we hear the conclusion. The gospel he preaches is very straightforward: save yourselves from a generation that has gone astray with false shepherds, a generation that killed Jesus Christ and rejected his teaching. But God has raised this Jesus from death and made him both Messiah and Lord. Jesus is the true shepherd who brings forgiveness of sins and eternal life.

In his speech Peter is addressing the Jews, but as we saw last week, the real audience is different. He is speaking to everyone, including us, those "still far off whom the Lord our God calls." We too are part of a generation led astray by an almost unlimited array of false shepherds, a generation in need of salvation, a generation so deeply shaken by war and problems and holocausts that we are left only to ask "What are we to do?"

Peter's answer to us is also very straightforward: "Reform and be baptized." But in our religious tradition, "reform" means much more than stopping after the third drink or watching our language. It means a complete turning about, a total change of heart. It means becoming new people. It means letting go of all the false shepherds and turning only to Christ, the true shepherd, and following his call alone. And to be baptized, as we have seen, means more than a social custom or a magical moment of grace. It means joining our shepherd in his mission, to live as he lived, and give as he gave, to follow his call into the grave so that we and others might rise with him to new life.

What are we to do? Peter's answer is simple: Follow the true shepherd through the gate of baptism. But hidden behind these simple words is a lifetime challenge for Easter living.

What false shepherds call to you today? How do Peter's words, "Reform and be baptized," apply to situations you face in your life right now? Where do you hear the voice of God?

WEDNESDAY

Responsorial Psalm: Psalm 23:1–3,3–4,5,6
"The Lord is my shepherd; I shall not want."

The first reading calls us to follow Christ our shepherd and to let our meeting with him in baptism be the gateway to new life. It is fitting, then, that we respond to this call with this most beloved of psalms, a psalm celebrating our shepherd and source of life, a psalm close to the heart of our Easter sacraments.

The early church sang this psalm at the Easter Vigil when the newly baptized and confirmed were being led in procession to the altar for the eucharist. For them the "verdant pastures" were the fields of paradise that we lost to sin, but which Christ restores to us. The "restful waters" were the waters of baptism, refreshing us with new life. The anointing with oil was the sealing with the Spirit in confirmation (see reflection for the Fifth Sunday of Easter), and the table spread before us and the overflowing cup meant the eucharistic banquet—the bread and wine that nourish us and give us life in the face of our great enemy, death. When we gather as a baptized people for our eucharistic assembly we sing this ancient song of faith to express our confident hope that the true shepherd is guiding us on right paths so that, even drawn into the midst of darkness, we will fear no evil. We sing this psalm to express our confident hope that God is strengthening us and giving us courage in our struggles to live as Christ lived. We sing this psalm to express our confident hope that Christ is leading us through the dark valley so that we too may dwell in the house of the Lord.

What dark valleys has Christ our shepherd led you through in your life? How have others brought the presence of Christ our shepherd to you? How have you been his presence for others?

THURSDAY

Second Reading: 1 Peter 2:20–25

"At one time you were straying like sheep but now you have returned to the shepherd, the guardian of your souls."

We have passed with Christ through the waters of baptism. We have sung a song of praise to Christ our shepherd. Now we listen as the author of First Peter tells us something about this shepherd and about ourselves.

Christ is our true shepherd, and can be easily distinguished from all the false shepherds because he does not leave us feeling trapped or abandoned. Christ followed the plan of God. Christ followed in the model of Isaiah's suffering servant (Isaiah 53:4–12). Christ is the true shepherd because he did not run away or throw blame or accusations or insults or threats. He did not try to escape and leave us to our fate. Christ is the true shepherd because he delivered himself up. He died for the sheep. He died so that we might live.

But the reading tells us much more. It tells us that we, too, are called to be true shepherds. In the waters of baptism we began the process of dying to ourselves so that we might live for

Christ, so that Christ might be our "example," so that we might "follow in his footsteps." We too are called to put up with the suffering that brings redemption, to take our part in the plan of God, to give and suffer for others, to work for reconciliation, to deliver ourselves up in our daily life so that others might have life in this world and in the next. By his wounds, we are healed. By our wounds, others are healed.

Such a difficult message may tempt us back to our false shepherds. But Christ has shown his truth with his blood. And in that truth we should rejoice, because "it was for this" that we "were called" into God's plan, and our true shepherd is the guardian of our souls.

What situation in your life needs God's healing? How is Christ calling you to be a true shepherd in your family? Your job? Your parish? Your neighborhood?

FRIDAY

Gospel: John 10:1–10

"I am the gate....The thief comes only to steal, slaughter and destroy. I came that they might have life and have it to the full."

The words we hear Jesus speak here are part of the story of the man born blind (John 9) that we proclaim on the Fourth Sunday of Lent. The blind man moved from darkness into light, and from spiritual darkness into the light of faith. But those who felt themselves sinless, those who had taken on the roles of shepherds and leaders of the people, remained trapped in darkness, unable to see who Jesus was.

Jesus' words here are aimed at those leaders and at us. When we try to lead or live by our own authority, when we act for our own profit, when we are more concerned with our own image than with the good of others, we are false shepherds who have listened to false shepherds—the thieves and marauders who promise salvation but bring only chaos and destruction.

But when we put others before ourselves, when we accept our sacrifices as part of God's plan of redemption, when we are truly interested in the sheep, when we remember our baptism and struggle to live as the changed people we have become, then we hear the voice of the true shepherd who walks in front of us and promises to keep us safe.

This is part of the promise and joy of Easter: Jesus Christ became one of us and died for us and rose for us—not to exploit us, not for his own good, not for his own glory—but to call us by name, to give us the freedom to live as the sons and daughters of a loving God. Christ alone is the gate into the pasture of God's love. He alone is the doorway that leads us out of the darkness of our traps and dead ends. He alone shows us the way through death into life.

Every day we face choices, and every day we hear the call of false shepherds beckoning to us with tempting but empty promises of salvation—do this, believe that, buy these. The man born blind judged his shepherds by comparing them to his encounter with Jesus. In the same way we must test our shepherds by comparing them to the Christ we meet in Scripture, in baptism, and in the eucharist, so that in the end we too can say, "Before I was blind, now I can see," and "Lord, I do believe."

What choices do you face today? In what ways do you feel trapped or at a dead end? In what ways can Christ be your gate into new freedom and new life? How does the shepherd call your name?

SATURDAY

The Liturgical Prayers

While I was writing these reflections, my wife and I took our son Michael to a nearby petting zoo, and Michael wanted to feed the sheep. There was a small coin-operated food dispenser in the zoo building. I took a coin out of my pocket, and a member of the flock, a big, woolly, smelly fellow, followed me to the dispenser. As I put the coin in he nudged me out of the way and stuck his mouth over the food slot, ready to gobble up the snack as soon as it appeared. I told him to get out the way. He ignored me. I pushed my leg against him. He pushed back. I put my hands on his side and shoved. He dug in. We battled for a few minutes, and in the end he won. He got the food, and I was left with a new appreciation for how tough and stubborn sheep can be. Shepherds don't have it as easy as I thought.

We've all seen the sentimental images of a gentle Jesus holding a perfectly coiffed lamb on his shoulder. Sentimentality is nice, but too much of it can pull us away from reality and make us think the shepherd has little to do with our real lives. We are, on the whole, a smelly, stubborn, selfish, tough-hearted people, not a gentle little lamb. And Christ is not a sentimental, dewy-eyed shepherd, but the presence among us of a loving, sacrificing God whose call brings us into the heart of life and death.

The prayers of the liturgy of the Fourth Sunday of Easter bring us back to this message of real life and death. We are, says the prayer after communion, a flock redeemed by *blood*. We pray in the opening prayer for the *courage* and the *strength* of Christ our shepherd. In the prayer over the gifts we pray that we may be restored, and that the continuing *work* of Christ might bring us joy.

The continuing work of Christ is dying to oneself to live for others. It is bringing reconciliation to the world, hospitality to strangers, healing and hope to the downcast, food to the hungry. It is bringing the kingdom of God. It is messy, tough, scary, and joyful work. And it is our work, for through the waters of baptism we are now the presence of Christ in our monotonous and exciting, joyful and sorrowful, and very real world.

What image comes to your mind when you think of Jesus the shepherd? What image comes to mind when you think of the waters of baptism? How is Christ the shepherd calling you to find Easter joy in your daily life?

Fourth Sunday of Easter

Water

For most of us who were baptized as infants, seeing the renewed rite of initiation celebrated in full splendor can come as something of a shock. It's not so much the novelty of seeing adults baptized or of hearing the new prayers and blessings. No, the shock comes in seeing how seriously the renewed rite takes the use of water and how wet and messy this new birth in the Spirit can be.

A few years ago I had the good fortune to participate in the Vigil celebration in a parish that took the use of water very seriously indeed. They had a new church building and they had been able to incorporate a baptismal pool into the architectural design. From where I sat in the assembly I could hear the water running in the pool. I could see the priest and catechumen wade into it. I could see the catechumen kneel in water up to his chest. And I watched in amazement as the priest began the baptismal formula and gently but firmly pushed the man's head under the water.

Three times he pushed him down, for Father, Son, and Spirit, and three times the man arose shivering and gasping for air with water cascading off him into the pool. By the time it was over there was water everywhere. The priest was soaked, the newly baptized man's hair dripped into his face, and water that had splashed out of the pool was running down the stone steps toward the assembly.

I was not the only one astonished. Everyone seemed to be angling for a better view. Cries of exclamation and amazement burst out of us as the man was dunked and then rose again. Not knowing how else to express the emotion building inside them, some people laughed nervously. For a few moments we felt strange, but very, very alive. The water seemed to fill us with a liberating, exhilarating energy and, when the moment ended, there was nothing to be done but explode into thunderous applause for this wet, dripping, tearful, joyful Christian whose birth into our midst we had been privileged to share.

I don't think you will forget the first time you see baptism celebrated this way. In a few parishes catechumens are submerged under the water. Far more frequently in parish practice, they have large quantities of water poured over them. And more and more parishes are building fonts that allow for the gentle immersion (up to the neck) of infants. But no matter the style, no matter whether the person to be baptized is an adult, a child, or an infant, the lavish use of water reveals truths about baptism that were easy to miss when our families gathered in the sacristy and a few drops of water were trickled over our heads. It is also helping us remember why water is such an important part of our Easter season.

Water is part of Easter because it speaks of life and of death. Life begins and thrives in water, but water also has a dark side that can destroy and drown.

Water is part of Easter because, through it, God touches our world. The Hebrew Scriptures speak often of water as the place of God's action in our midst. In the very beginning, God's spirit breathed on the waters of creation. God sent the destroying flood. God gave the Israelites life-giving water flowing from a desert rock. But the most important passage, for Jews and Christians alike, is the crossing of the Reed Sea when God gave the Israelites life by drowning their Egyptian oppressors.

For Christians, God's presence in our world is summed up in Jesus, the living water, who was baptized in the Jordan and received the Spirit, who cured a blind man through water, who washed the feet of his disciples, who had water flow from his pierced and crucified body, and who said that no one could enter God's kingdom without being born of water and the Spirit.

The waters of baptism can speak powerfully of these images

of death and life, and life from death. The font is the water of creation alive with God's Spirit. It is the watery grave from the flood in which your old self was *drowned* (that's what *baptizesthai* means in Greek) so that you might receive the Spirit. It was your passage through the sea with Christ so that you might escape the bondage of sin and live in the promised land of God's kingdom. It was the dark and cold tomb in which you were buried with Christ so that you might share in his resurrection. It was the bath in which you were washed clean so that you might in turn wash and serve others. It is the messy, wet womb in which you came to birth in Christ. It is the water from his side, refreshing and nurturing you and your assembly and helping you grow into the gathering of his body.

When you come to Mass, take special notice of the baptismal font and how water is used in your parish. If it is used lavishly, bring your memories of it to the gathering. If it is used sparingly, a few drops at a time, remember what the water means. In either case, rejoice in the water. It is the exhilarating, terrifying, and joyful touch of God.

Toward the Fifth Sunday of Easter

Acts 6:1–7
Psalm 33:1–2,4–5,18–19
1 Peter 2:4–9
John 14:1–12

MONDAY

I'm never quite sure how I feel about our church. I go back and forth between loving it and hating it, being proud of it and embarrassed by it. It has challenged me and given me room to grow. It has brought me comfort in times of loneliness and sorrow, but it has also infuriated me with its insensitivity. I always listen to what the church has to say, but sometimes I think that what it has to say is worthy of being ignored. I feel connected to the church and yet I often feel like a stranger. It brings joy into my life, but my family is where I feel I most fully belong.

I've been a member of parishes where I was treated like a VIP, and of other parishes where all they wanted was an envelope in the basket. I've had parish staff members treat me with respect, and others who turned and walked away when I was in the middle of a sentence. I've seen parishes work together beautifully, and I've been on parish councils that have broken into hating factions worthy of the Middle East.

For me, belonging to the church means being at home with tension and mixed emotions. And I don't think I'm the only person who feels this way. I think there are a lot of us who want to be much more than "cultural Catholics," but who aren't quite sure how to be fully at home with our parishes and our church. We can find joy in our struggle, but we can also be left wondering why we have to have a church in the first place.

Easter is a time to ponder and celebrate the church's mysterious, ambiguous presence in our lives. Our readings this week cannot save us from tension and struggle, nor do they give us a full doctrinal understanding of the church, but they can give us some central insights into its life and mission and help us remember who we are and why we are here.

As you reflect on the readings, think about yourself and the church. How big a role does it play in your life? When you think of the church, what image comes to mind? What kind of church are you called to belong to? And how do you belong? Why is the presence of the church something to celebrate?

TUESDAY

First Reading: Acts 6:1–7
"The ones who spoke Greek complained that their widows were being neglected."

At first glance, a reading about conflict and tension in the church might not seem to fit in with a season of Easter joy, but this, too, is a story of dying and rising. Behind it all seems to be the church's developing break with Judaism. The church was getting larger and, as human beings always seem to do, the people were siding with their own kind against the strangers. The idyllic community Luke described to us a few weeks ago was breaking down into factions. If things went too far the body of Christ would be ripped apart.

But the early church survived its conflict because it remembered that harmony and unity are what the body of Christ must always strive for. They solved their problem in a way that involved and respected the gifts of every member of the community. They were even willing to change their structure to adapt to new needs, and they emerged with a new group of ministers and new life for their mission in the world.

Conflict and tension are facts of life in our church. They can destroy us, or we can do what the early church did. We can strive for unity in diversity. We can remember that sharing all things in common, welcoming strangers, proclaiming the word, serving others, respecting and nurturing the gifts of others, and working for reconciliation are at the *heart* of being the body of Christ. They flow from the life of Christ himself. We can remember that church structure, from pope to parish council subcommittee, exists, not to hold power, but only so that the unity of the body may be maintained, that the life of the community may be nurtured, and that every member of the church may be free and empowered to participate in the mission of bringing the peace of the risen Christ to the world.

If we can do this, and if we, too, can root our response in "prayer and the ministry of the word," then perhaps the tensions we feel now will become resurrection stories to tell our children.

How does your parish handle conflict? Whom do you need to be reconciled with right now?

WEDNESDAY

Responsorial Psalm: Psalm 33:1–2,4–5,18–19
"Of the kindness of the Lord the earth is full."

In the first reading we heard a story of the dying and rising of the body of Christ. Now, as a people, we respond as we should to any resurrection story—with a song of joyful praise.

We sing of how the early church put its faith in God and how God preserved them. We sing of all the times God's mercy has been felt in our world, most especially in the paschal mystery of Christ. We sing of our hope that God's eyes will be upon us in our own time of need, that God will walk with us through death and famine to a new rising. For we, too, place our trust in God's justice and kindness.

Above all, we sing the praises of our God because that is what our church is called to do. With the Jews we are a sign to the world of what God is doing in its midst. As the second reading this week reminds us, we have been called "to proclaim the glorious works" of the God who called us from darkness into light.

This is why the church exists: to proclaim God's glorious works by reaching out with the healing power of God's word, by being an active sign of God's justice, by preserving from famine and death, and by letting the world know, not just by what we sing but by what we do, that "of the kindness of the Lord the earth is full." We are in the world so that the world may come to know this God and join our work of giving thanks and chanting praise.

In what ways does your parish reach out to others? In what ways do you sing the praises of our God?

THURSDAY

Second Reading: 1 Peter 2:4–9
"You too are living stones."

When we join together to sing a song of praise, several things seem to happen naturally. We feel more alive. We feel closer together. We can be inspired to see ourselves as a people with a mission. We can be inspired to take action.

In this way, singing this Sunday's responsorial psalm may prepare us to hear this second reading. It may prepare us to think of ourselves not as individuals, but as a community that has become "a chosen race, a royal priesthood, a consecrated nation," a people with a mission. It may give us the courage to dare to think of ourselves as "living stones."

We may need the responsorial psalm to get us ready to hear these words because they are not easy words to hear. We might think of "chosen race, royal priesthood, consecrated nation" as making us special, in the same way we think of the specific ordained priesthood within the community as something special and set apart. But, before anything else, both the ordained priesthood and the priesthood of all believers begin in baptism and are rooted in the same place—the priesthood of Christ. And Christ's priesthood is not rooted in status, but in sacrifice and service to others.

The author of First Peter does not call us a chosen race, a royal priesthood, a consecrated nation because we enjoy a higher status or have special privileges that come from being the Lord's anointed. The author uses this language to suggest that our baptism puts special demands upon us.

We can't leave the work of Christ to others. We are not lifeless pieces of rock cemented into a dull church wall. We are a church of living stones, alive through baptism and eucharist, filled with the life of the Spirit, chosen and set apart only so that we may break down barriers. We are called to let our daily lives proclaim to the world the glory of our God.

The daily concern we show one another, how we handle our responsibilities, and the small ways we bring justice and forgiveness to the world are all opportunities to be living stones. How is God calling you to carry on the work of Christ?

FRIDAY

Gospel: John 14:1–12
"I am the way, and the truth, and the life."

When I was growing up, whenever I heard the words Jesus speaks in the opening verses of this gospel passage I thought of heaven. Jesus was leaving, the disciples were sad, and he was promising to go and prepare a place for them in his Father's house, which, I had been taught, was heaven. This house had many dwelling places, and that, of course, meant that heaven was big enough for lots and lots of people.

I wasn't the only person to think this way, and the early church seemed to share my interpretation. They expected Jesus to return very soon and take them to heaven.

But the early church grew up and realized that Jesus was talking about more than heaven here. They came to realize that we, the living stones, are the many dwelling places of God, all built into the "Father's house" upon the cornerstone of Christ. They came to see that Christ is so deeply rooted in God that he doesn't merely prepare the way to God, he *is* the way, that

Christ doesn't merely reveal truths about God, he *is* the truth, and that Christ doesn't merely tell us about the life of God, he *is* that life itself. They came to see that Christ is still with us through the gift of the Spirit. They came to see that Christ's saving work continues in the community that is now his body. They came to see that our faith in Christ would allow us to do what Christ did "and far greater than these." They came to see that his life of self-offering love is now ours to spread to every corner of the world.

Through our baptism, and in the power of the Spirit, we are to bring Christ to the world so that the world may see God. How does the world see God through you?

SATURDAY

The Liturgical Prayers

I know a doctor who donated her first year after residency to providing medical care to the homeless. I know a husband and wife who, in spite of their own ill-health and physical disabilities, spend several hours a week looking after older neighbors. I know a business executive who offers his services as a handyman free to the poor and elderly who cannot provide for themselves. I know a family that fasts one day every week and sends the money they save to the poor. I know of parishes where the people bring food items for the poor as part of their Sunday Mass offering. I know a woman who drives a crotchety old neighbor to church and to the store every day, knowing she will never be thanked for these acts of kindness. I know a man who turned down a promotion because it would drastically cut down on the time he could spend with his kids. I met a woman going from house to house in freezing weather and getting doors slammed in her face, all to pass out literature for a justice and peace organization.

You and I both know lots of people like this. And many of them are average, ordinary Catholics bringing the church to the world.

Our ordinary lives are full of opportunities for service. Even taking pride in our work and loving our families can be acts of worship, holy endeavors of a priestly people who reveal the face of Christ.

As our church gathers on the Fifth Sunday of Easter, we pray, as we pray every Sunday, to be changed ever more fully into a people who can bring Christ to the world. In the opening prayer we pray for true freedom and our promised inheritance—not just "heaven," but the spiritual freedom to take our share in Christ's life. In the prayer over the gifts we pray that *"everything we do* may be directed by a knowledge of God's truth"—and that truth is the dying and rising Christ. In the prayer after communion we pray that our communal celebration may give us new purpose and new life, through Christ, who is the way and the life for us all.

When you say Amen to these prayers, what will they mean in your life? How is Christ calling you to be his presence in the world?

Fifth Sunday of Easter

Oil

Before you were born, you knew your mother. You rested and fed and played and grew in her, all warm and easy and secure. You listened to her heart beat. You picked up her emotions, her joys, and her fears. You may even have learned to recognize her voice, to feel her arms embracing you as she wrapped them around herself, and to respond to that touch of love with a dancing kick or a playful turn.

After birth you still longed for such tenderness. The caress that soothed you, the kiss that warmed you, the hug that held you secure—all these and countless other gestures and whisperings (or their lack) let you know what the world was like, and what love you might expect to find there.

Even now, as an adult, have things really changed? Even those of us who aren't "huggy, kissy" people long for the touch of love. We need the spouse's kiss that delights and comforts, the friend's embrace that warms the heart, and the child's hug that turns a day's worry into joy. We have a human need for all the embraces and touches that can do so much to calm our fears, console our grief, soothe our aches, destroy our enmity, end our loneliness, and give us strength when nothing else will do.

And it is the same when we approach our God. God made us human beings, not angels. We have bodies and we live in a sensual world of touch, taste, smell, sight, and sound. Thinking about God's love is not enough. We need to touch and be touched by God. We need to feel God's love in our world. We need God's touch to bring us strength and comfort. We need the embrace that floods us with God's love.

Deeply rooted in the human need to touch God and be

touched by God is the Easter symbol found in the use of oil. It may be hard for us to see this oil as the touch of God. We think of oil as something to put on salads or in our cars. But our use of oil is rooted in the five thousand years of our Christian and Jewish heritage, and in our simple human gestures of caring and touching.

For ancient peoples, oil had many uses and many meanings. It was used for bathing in the way we would use soap, and as an after bath adornment. It was used as a salve to soothe and comfort the skin. It was burned in lamps to give light, and used in religious rituals. In times of trouble it was often a luxury item and its use conveyed a sense of festivity, fullness, and abundance. It was poured over the heads of priests, prophets, and kings to show that God's Spirit was now poured out upon them, that they were now dedicated to the special service of God and God's people, that they had become sacred persons, that God was with them and would strengthen them, and that they had become the Lord's anointed.

In Hebrew, the word for the Anointed One is *Messiah*. In Greek, the word is *Christ*. For Christians, Jesus is truly *the* Anointed One, the Christ, the Messiah, the one foretold and longed for. He was baptized and received the Spirit. In him, "priest," "prophet," and "king" received the fullness of their meaning. He is High Priest, interceding with God on our behalf and leading us in worship. He is Prophet, revealing to us the thoughts and words and presence of God. He is King, who has been superexalted in glory because he humbled himself, obediently accepting death, that we might live. Through Christ, we see and hear and touch our God.

But we also know that Christ lives today in the gathering of his followers. The Spirit reveals that we are the body of Christ. In baptism and confirmation we have had oil poured upon us. We are also the anointed ones.

The oil poured upon you in baptism carried with it all these rich meanings. Your anointing before baptism was a sign of love and comfort from the community. It was the community's embrace, signifying that you were now its child too, and that it would help to protect you and care for you, and nurture your new life in God. It was an oil of cleansing, to drive out the spirit of darkness that plagues us all so that room might be made in you for the burning light of God's holy Spirit. It was God's touch, bringing strength so that you might endure the trials that your new life calls you to. It was God's promise that you do not take the journey of discipleship alone.

Your anointing after baptism was a sign, like the water, that you have been touched and claimed by God, that God's holy Spirit has indeed been lavishly poured out upon you. The fragrance of the oil was but a hint of the sweet presence of the Spirit now living within you.

When you come to Mass today, you may not see anyone use oil, but you will see and touch the Lord's anointed—the catechumens strengthened with oil on their way to the font, the newly baptized still basking in the fragrance of new life in the Spirit, your neighbors and strangers, your family, and you. You have all been anointed. You all share in Christ's risen life as priest, prophet, and king.

The use of natural things like water and oil shows us that God does not make abstract promises. It shows that our mission to live as Christ lived begins *here*, in this natural world, in the day to day activity of our lives. Behold, said St. Paul, now is the acceptable time. *Now* is the day of salvation.

So let the promises of the oil begin to take root in you now. Gather around the Lord's table as a community that nurtures, cares, protects, and lives in the Spirit. Take the strength that comes from that gathering and dare to be the presence of Christ living and active in your created world. Bring to the world the joy of God's kiss. Bring to the world the strength of God's embrace, that it too may know where its life comes from, and what kind of love it can expect to find there.

Toward the Sixth Sunday of Easter

Acts 8:5–8,14–17
Psalm 66:1–3,4–5,6–7,16,20
1 Peter 3:15–18
John 14:15–21

MONDAY

I wanted to be a father. When Deborah was pregnant I read all the books and made all the plans a father-to-be makes. I was prepared for fatherhood. But I was not prepared for Michael.

It wasn't the sleepless nights or the other changes a baby brings. I was ready for all of that, and took them in stride. What I wasn't ready for was how distant I felt from him. I carried on like any good dad, and when I held my son, I felt warm and protective, but that seemed so little compared to how intimately and joyously connected Michael and Deborah seemed to be. Shouldn't I be feeling more? Where was the love my heart should be bursting with? Where was this bonding they all talk about? Why didn't I feel more connected to this newborn?

Deborah comforted me and told me that connections take time. So I patiently did my fatherly duties and shared my family's life, hoping at least that in my love for my wife I could share her love for our son. And over the months of changing and cleaning and feeding and sharing, the wonderful thing did happen. I got to know Michael, and I grew to love him, and our connections grow stronger every day. In the giving and caring of family life, I stopped being in love with fatherhood and fell in love with my son.

I wanted you to know this about me, because I think many of us take the same approach to Christian discipleship. We read the books and know the rules. We fall in love with the idea of being disciples. But we forget that, before anything else, Christian discipleship is coming to know and love a person—Jesus Christ.

The readings for year A of the Sixth Sunday of Easter beckon us deeper into this loving encounter with Christ, and deeper into our understanding of the church, for we come to know and love Christ through his Spirit, and we encounter the Spirit most clearly by living in a community that is filled with its life.

As you pray with these readings, think of your own family, friends, and parish. Think of how you come to know and love others. Think about the Spirit in your life. Think of how you can come more deeply to know and love Christ.

TUESDAY

First Reading: Acts 8:5–8,14–17
"The two went down to these people and prayed that they might receive the Holy Spirit."

It may be hard for us to see ourselves in this reading. We have parishes, deaneries, dioceses, and local, national, and international organizations of just about everything in the church. We have theological systems and religious education curricula. We belong to a church that has had two thousand years to develop its structure.

We are so organized, in fact, that we are often tempted to think it's always been this way. So when we read this passage from Acts, we tend to see Luke speaking about the difference between baptism and confirmation as if a couple of bishops squeezed Samaria into their Spring confirmation schedule.

But most Scripture scholars are coming to agree that Luke, like the rest of the early church, knew nothing of a separate sacrament of confirmation. That came later for many different reasons. What Luke is really getting at here is the *connection* between Jerusalem and Samaria, between Samaria and your parish, between Peter and John and you. That connection is the Spirit.

From the apostolic church in Jerusalem onward, we have never been bonded together by the expulsion of shrieking unclean spirits, or by rejoicing that rises to fever pitch, or even by our structure and organization, no matter how helpful these might be. We are a people, a church, linked by a common vision, a common love of Christ whom we experience in the Spirit.

We know what the Spirit is by seeing something of what the Spirit does. The Spirit reveals Christ. The Spirit makes us the one body of Christ and builds up the church. The Spirit links us to each other, to Christ, and thus to God. The Spirit gives us the faith to love, to pray, to dare—as a community and as individuals—to be Christ's presence in the world.

How do you see the Spirit alive in your parish and in your life? How closely linked do you feel to all the Christians who have come before you and who will come after you?

WEDNESDAY

Responsorial Psalm: Psalm 66:1–3,4–5,6–7,16,20
"Come and see the works of God."

One of the gifts of the Spirit is to recognize and give praise to our God, and that is what the church invites us to do in response to our first reading this week. We join with the people of Israel to celebrate the tremendous deeds of our God, the God who led the Israelites through the sea to safety, the God who leads us through the waters of baptism to a share in the Spirit and to the gift of life.

Singing this song of Israel reminds us again of connections. For we are linked not just to other Christians back to the apostles, but to the larger tradition of those who recognized the Spirit of God moving over the waters, who found God revealed in their history, whose prophets anticipated the outpouring of the Spirit on God's people, and in whose midst Jesus of Nazareth was nurtured and finally revealed as the Christ of God.

We are, in a special way, one large family, a people so filled with God's love that we can do nothing but rejoice in it and proclaim it in all our victories and failures and dyings and risings. We are a people called to be the visible works of God so that all the earth may recognize that it too is part of this family, that it too is called to be connected in God's Spirit. We are called to be the visible works of God until all the earth knows that it, too, has a reason to cry out to God with joy.

How wide is your spiritual family? Do you feel connected to others outside of the Catholic church? How will your works give praise to God today?

THURSDAY

Second Reading: 1 Peter 3:15–18
"He was given life in the realm of the Spirit."

When we were baptized and confirmed, we took our place in the long connected line of disciples, the church, the People of God who have breathed the Spirit from generation to generation. And here in this church family, the Spirit was poured out upon us as well, so that we too might come to know and love Christ, so that Christ might live in us.

The second reading this week encourages us to cooperate in this work of the Spirit. Speaking to the newly initiated, as well as to us, the author of First Peter reveals the kind of life the Spirit brings. In the life of the Spirit we come to know Christ by living his life. We do not return insult for insult or libel for libel. Life in the Spirit is spent in pursuit of justice, but it is also marked by gentleness and respect, no matter how little respect we might get in return. Like Christ, who died "a just man for the sake of the unjust," our life in the Spirit is a life lived for others. It is a life that should never give in to despair, for through all our difficulties and persecutions, and through all our daily dyings and risings, Christ leads us to God.

It is not an easy life, this life in the Spirit. For two thousand years, men and women and the church family as a whole have struggled with it, now cooperating with the Spirit, now standing in its way. But through all our family ups and downs, the same

Spirit has stayed with us, still breathing the presence and love of Christ into our hearts, still calling us together to life in its realm.

How is the Spirit of the risen Christ speaking to you in your family and in your parish? What signs of the Spirit have you found in your life? How is the Spirit calling you to share in Christ's life?

FRIDAY

Gospel: John 14:15–21
"I will not leave you orphaned."

Unless we are frustrated parents dealing with a stubborn child, obedience is not a word most of us seem to like these days. And yet here in this gospel Jesus speaks of obedience not once but twice. And both times the obedience is connected to love.

In speaking this way, Christ is echoing the God of Israel whose life he shares, the God who established a covenant with Israel, the God who linked love and obedience in that covenant. (See, for example, Deuteronomy 6:5 and Wisdom 6:18.) The people of Israel are to keep God's commandments, and the greatest of these is to love God with all their hearts, souls, and strength (Deuteronomy 6:5). In exchange, they would have God's love and be God's people.

Christ makes a similar covenant with us. We are to love Christ, and prove that we love him by obeying his commands.

But obeying his commands goes far beyond moral precepts and thou-shalt-nots. His command to us is to be new people, to share his life, and to "love one another" as he has loved us (John 15:12). And if we do this, then Christ promises that we will share his love and be his people.

Even though Christ is preparing to depart, he proclaims in this covenant that he will not abandon us or leave us orphaned. He will share with us the Spirit, who will dwell within us and our community, who will bring Christ back to us. The Spirit will bring us so closely into communion with Christ that we can truly share in the love, plan, and very life of God.

Christ speaks to us not as disobedient children, but as the sons and daughters—the church family—of the same God he called his Father. Christ calls us, not to a set of laws, but to a covenant, a covenant that, above all else, calls us to love Christ. If we are faithful to this covenant, then Christ will stay close to us in the Spirit, and reveal himself ever more fully to us. In this way our love for him and our share in his life will grow, and in the power of that same Spirit, our own words and deeds will reveal Christ more fully to the world.

How is Christ calling you to obey his commands? How are you coming to know and love Christ? How is Christ revealing himself to you through the Spirit?

SATURDAY

The Liturgical Prayers

We've been told all our lives that we should love Jesus. We've read stories of saints whose love for Jesus is the stuff of legends. We have pictures and prayers and hymns and songs that make loving Christ seem as simple as pasting a "Honk if you love Jesus" bumper sticker on our cars.

But the liturgy of the Sixth Sunday of Easter pulls us back to a deeper meaning. The readings and prayers remind us that true love is expressed not in bumper stickers or saccharine songs, but in sacrifice. They remind us that we ultimately come to love someone not by talking about it, but by getting to know them, by being connected to them, by sharing their ups and downs, by living our real life with theirs.

For most of us that love grows first in our families. Real families aren't perfect. They have their times of joy and times of sorrow, their times of peace and their times of war. And our families live or die not by how often we say "I love you" to each other (though that never hurts), but by how well we come to understand each other, tolerate each other's failings, sacrifice for, support, and love each other—not in theory, but in practice.

The same is true for our church. On Sunday we gather in the Spirit as a Christian family, connected to every other Christian family from the beginning to the end of time. We join together to remember Christ, not just to talk about him. We join together so that we might share his life, so that we may come to know and love him in our daily lives—not in theory, but in practice.

So in our opening prayer for this Sixth Sunday of Easter, we pray that we might "express *in our lives* the love we celebrate." In the alternate opening prayer we pray that we might share in Christ's *loving sacrifice*. And in the prayer after communion we pray that we might be strengthened by the love of our Easter gathering so that we might feel its saving power in our *daily* life—not in theory, not in sentiment, but in practice.

What do you learn of Christ in your parish's eucharistic gathering? What does loving Christ mean in your daily life?

Sixth Sunday of Easter

The Paschal Candle

When the Christian community gathers on Holy Saturday night, its first experience of the Easter rites is not of water, not of oil, but of darkness. Men and women stand holding on to unlit candles in a space that's familiar and yet so very strange. Darkness makes everything different. They hear coughing and whispering, but all they see are shapes and shadows. Their eyes strain against the darkness and they may instinctively move closer to their loved ones as if seeking mutual protection and comfort in the blackness of the night.

In the dark the assembly stands, uncertain and waiting, waiting as a formless, dark world waited on the first day of creation, waiting for God to bring order out of chaos, waiting for those very first words our tradition attributes to God: "Let there be light."

"Let there be light." We use it as a cliché. Persons flip light switches and call out with pompous solemnity "Let there be light." In our world, light is easily available, and its very abundance can keep us from remembering how important it is to us and why it plays such a central role in our Easter celebrations.

Our ancestors knew no such luxury. For them, darkness ruled the night, and with it came the cold, hidden dangers, and confusion. The rising of the sun was a time of rejoicing, for it meant that warmth and order and at least a measure of security had returned to their world. For them, light and dark carried many of the meanings of human existence—the rhythm of day and night, safety and fear, hope and despair, knowledge and ignorance, wisdom and foolishness, victory and defeat, knowing the way and getting lost—even birth and death.

We still use the language of light and dark to express these things today, and light is as important to us as it was to our ancestors. In a recent year, for example, people in the U.S. spent over $17 billion on electrical lighting equipment, and over $15 billion just for the electricity to light their homes. In urban areas around the globe, we create a world so full of nighttime light that it obscures the stars, but anyone who has ever hesitated to walk down an unlit city street or who has been in a power blackout in a storm knows what our ancestors knew—that darkness can be the place of danger where the evil one roams freely.

It's only when we are thrown into the dark that we can understand why ancient peoples would welcome and rejoice in the light of a single flickering candle or lamp, why they would greet it with the expression, "Hail, friendly light," and why groups of Christians gathering for prayer every evening for almost two thousand years have sung the *Phos hilaron,* "O Radiant Light," the hymn of praise to Christ, the true light who dispels the darkness of our lives.

It is in this tradition of yearning for Christ our light that we stand in the dark on Vigil night. We stand with generations of Christians who came before us. We come with all our fears and hopes, our joys and sorrows, our attempts at order and the chaos that results from them. We come with all the violence, sin, and selfishness that darken our lives. We bring them all to a place as dark as a tomb, a world in need of new birth and resurrection, and we wait for the light.

And then in the darkness a fire is lit and from the fire a candle. When that candle is brought into the church, who among us can stand unmoved at the sight of that single brilliant flame piercing the blackness around us? Here is the risen Christ, the "light that shines in the darkness," "the light of the world" who came, the Scriptures tell us, to light a fire on the earth so that we might be "rescued from darkness" and "walk in the light." Here before us is the Christ who is "God from God, light from light." Whoever believes in him cannot remain in darkness but will share in the light of life.

Our share in this light comes to us in baptism. In the early church, baptism was called *photisma*, "illumination." Jesus himself says that we are the light of the world. In baptism we become children of light, called in the Spirit to let the light of the risen Christ shine in our hearts. And just as the light of that single paschal candle is passed to all our smaller candles until the church is ablaze with light, so too by our baptism we are called to combine our share of the light with other lights in the body of Christ, until the darkness of the world is burned away.

Our share in that work will cost us, as it cost Christ, for the grains of incense in the candle signify the wounds of crucifixion. The candle represents darkness and death as well as light and life. The risen Christ is the crucified Christ, and the date cut into the candle is not the date of Christ's historical dying and rising, it is *our* year, *our* time, the time of Christ's dying and rising *in us*.

When the Jews were wandering, lost and dispirited in the desert, God sent a pillar of fire to comfort them in the darkness and lead them on to the promised land. Today at Mass, the burning paschal candle still goes before the assembly like that pillar of fire, calling all of us out of darkness and deeper into the paschal mystery, urging us to illuminate a world darkened by injustice and despair, and leading us through the Spirit along the path of Christ, who showed us that dying to self and living for others is the only way to live in the light.

Toward the Seventh Sunday of Easter

Acts 1:12–14
Psalm 27:1,4,7–8
1 Peter 4:13–16
John 17:1–11

MONDAY

Right across the river from our town is the factory that makes Trident submarines. A lot of my neighbors build these submarines. Others have been arrested for protesting against them. Some say these subs exist only to fight immoral wars and their huge cost steals food from the poor. Others say they are an important deterrent to war, part of a nuclear strategy that has kept the peace between superpowers for forty-five years.

Should we build them or not? Should we work there or not? These submarines are an important issue around here, an issue involving real-life choices about jobs and families, patriotism and discipleship. It's an issue that could even divide parishes, for I've heard sermons for both sides, sermons that assure us that Jesus would agree with this viewpoint or that.

I usually get very uncomfortable with people who are sure they know exactly what Jesus would do or say on a given issue. In the gospels, Jesus is always surprising people. He never seemed to be where they thought he would be and they were often amazed at whom they'd find him talking to. And even in the first reading for the Ascension (which is celebrated in this Easter week), the apostles, having lived with Jesus through his ministry, passion, and resurrection, still ask, "Lord, are you going to restore the rule to Israel now?" After all that time, they still didn't know who Jesus was.

It's very human to believe that God wants what we want. It's very easy to find Scripture texts that back up our actions, lifestyle, or point of view. But life isn't black and white. Christ is usually calling us to some kind of change, and if God's will were so easy to figure out, then God would never have needed to give us the Spirit.

We're close to Pentecost now, and once again our readings focus on the church and the Spirit. They remind us that we must live our lives as people of the Spirit—in the world, but not of it. They remind us that it is only by opening ourselves to that Spirit and dwelling in its light that we can come to understand how God is acting in our lives, and what real-life choices the risen Christ is calling us to make.

What is Christ calling you to face or rethink? How can you move more deeply into the life of the Spirit?

TUESDAY

First Reading: Acts 1:12–14
"Together they devoted themselves to constant prayer."

Jesus prayed. Before he received the holy Spirit at his baptism, he paused to pray (Luke 3:21). Before choosing his disciples, he spent the night in prayer (Luke 6:12). Jesus was at prayer when the transfiguration occurred (Luke 9:28). And he prayed before his arrest and crucifixion (Luke 22:41). Luke often shows Jesus praying about his mission, praying to decide what to do, and praying about his community.

Now, after the Ascension, Luke gives us a picture of that community. The risen Christ has left them, but he has also given them a mission. So what do they do? Like Jesus, they pray.

They gather in the upper room that is their hiding place, their place away from the world. They wait there and they pray—not as individuals, but as a full community of men and women. *Together* they wait and pray for God to act, for God to guide them, for God to give them the Spirit.

When that Spirit comes, they will be changed people. They will burst out of that upper room and move boldly into the world, knowing that they are guided by the Spirit. But first they pray.

We are the continuation of that community. We are as directly connected to it as it was to Christ. Their mission is now our mission. We are the heirs to the Spirit that filled their life. But that Spirit is not a gift to take for granted. It's a gift that we must constantly seek, a gift that we must constantly open ourselves up to, a gift to be prayed for.

So we gather in our communities, our equivalents of the upper room. We don't gather in order to waste time, run away from the world, ignore our mission, or come away with a tidbit of religious instruction. We gather to pray for the gift of the Spirit, so that we might praise God, know Christ, and let the wisdom of the Spirit guide us boldly back into the world. It all begins with prayer.

Does your community see itself as praying for the gift of the Spirit? How important is prayer in your life?

WEDNESDAY

Responsorial Psalm: Psalm 27:1,4,7–8
"This I seek: To dwell in the house of the Lord all the days of my life."

The first reading shows us a community waiting for God to guide them. Before they begin their mission, they pray to God for the gift of Christ's Spirit.

Perhaps in their prayer they sang this psalm. It would have well expressed their prayer that God would not abandon them. It is filled with the hope that God would hear the sound of their call and be their light and their salvation.

Now gathered in our community we too sing to God about our need for the Spirit. We sing of our hope that God will have pity on us and answer us with the Spirit, who will help us to see and know Christ. We sing, and we pray, that the Spirit may enlighten us so that we may gaze on the loveliness of the Lord.

We shouldn't sing this song as a fearful or timid people. We know that God has rescued us and will do so again. We believe that the Spirit of God will reveal good things to us and bring us into the land of the living. We are a people who know that we can do nothing without God, but we sing of our hope that God will have pity on us and be our refuge. We are a people of hopeful prayer. We pray that God will give us the one thing we ask for, and that all good gifts will flow from that. We pray for the Spirit to dwell in us so that we may dwell in the house of the Lord forever.

Is the Spirit of Christ the "one thing" you ask of God? What gifts have you received from the Spirit to bring to your community?

THURSDAY

Second Reading: 1 Peter 4:13–16
"Rejoice insofar as you share Christ's sufferings."

Some of the choices the Spirit calls us to make can be very costly in our lives. They might mean the loss of a job, or a friend, or a certain kind of reputation. They might mean letting go of a part of the world we have grown to like very much. They might mean facing things we've managed to avoid or growing in ways that we find very painful.

But, like the original hearers of Peter's first letter, we are risen people. We have passed through the waters of baptism. We have followed Christ into the grave so that we might rise with him to new life.

So we pray for the gift of his Spirit. We pray for the Spirit who will help us see clearly what Christ is calling us to do, the Spirit who will make us so confident of our mission that we can see the cost of discipleship as a reason for rejoicing.

When we persevere in prayer, God will give us the Spirit and the courage to discern how the Spirit's voice is heard in our community. Over a lifetime of such

ASCENSION

Acts 1:1–11
Psalm 47:2–3,6–7,8–9
Ephesians 1:17–23
Matthew 28:16–20

prayer, the Spirit will help us see the many ways that we are all murderers, thieves, malefactors, and the destroyer of the rights of others. The Spirit will keep showing us the example of Christ. The Spirit will give us the courage to begin to live Christ's life.

Today, on the Feast of the Ascension, Christ urges us to get on with our mission in this world. That mission isn't easy, and none of us wants to suffer for being a Christian. But we have the example of Christ and the promise of the Spirit. And in that Spirit we can pray and sing with hope the words of this Sunday's responsorial psalm: "The Lord is my life's refuge; of whom should I be afraid?"

What are you afraid of in your life? How can your sufferings be cause for rejoicing? What mission is Christ calling you to?

FRIDAY

Gospel: John 17:1–11
"I pray for them. I will no longer be in the world, but they will be in the world."

In the first reading, the Christian community stands between the Ascension and Pentecost. They are caught between one action of God and another. They have been commissioned to bring Christ to the world, but they still haven't received the power to carry that mission out. Something is over, but what comes next is not yet completely clear. So they wait. At moments like this, sometimes all we can do is wait and pray.

Jesus is at a similar point in this gospel. His earthly mission is at an end. His "hour," the time for his passion, death, resurrection, and ascension, has come. He has done the work of his Father. Now he waits for something new to begin. And he prays.

As we might expect, he prays above all for his mission and his community. He first asks for glory from his Father, not for himself, but so that he might bestow eternal life on his disciples. He then prays directly for the disciples, for those of us who are in the world, but who really belong to God.

The way John presents this passage, we can see what a close connection there is between Jesus and God, between Father and Son. Indeed, the connection is so tight, so intimate, that when we know Jesus we know God. Jesus has made the glory of the Father visible to the world.

But there is more here. We have been given to Christ by God. The intimacy Christ shares with the Father is ours to share with Christ in the Spirit. In the Spirit, we glorify Jesus by making his origins and his power and his life visible to the world.

Christ has entrusted his message to us. We know where he came from and where he went. Now we, his church, continue his work in the world through the power of the Spirit. What do we do first? We pray.

What situations in your life do you need to bring to prayer? What kinds of things does your community pray for?

SATURDAY

The Liturgical Prayers

It is not easy to be a disciple of Jesus in this world—not even during the fifty days of Easter. This time, above all, we celebrate resurrection and forgiveness and we yearn for the heaven that is our true home.

But we are not in heaven, and Scripture tells us again and again to get our heads out of the clouds. While we are children of God, ultimately to share in God's life forever, that glory is yet to be fully revealed. In the meantime, our mission is here. We are to live out our dyings and risings in the world of our daily lives.

This is an Easter message. It is a message of great joy because we share in the mission of our God—to live a life for others, to be a special sign of God's presence in our world, to do our part in the long line of disciples until the whole world is swept up into the joy of God's love.

So we stay here, and we make the hard decisions and the difficult choices, and like everyone else we suffer the trials and tribulations of being human. But deep down we can rejoice, for Christ has promised to be with us in his Spirit, and the Spirit can help us transform our sorrows into joys.

Sometimes it's hard to see this clearly when life is being cold, lonely, and cruel. Sometimes there is nothing else to do but pray.

In the opening prayer of the liturgy of the Seventh Sunday of Easter, for example, we ask God for nothing but to help us remember that Christ has promised to remain with us until the end of time. The eucharistic prayer, as always, tells us the meaning of all our dyings and risings, and the prayer after communion asks that what we have celebrated may give us hope that we will share in Christ's glory.

Christ has promised to be with us. And in the alternative opening prayer we ask that Christ's presence among us may lead us to a vision of unlimited truth and unfold for us the beauty of God's love.

Who could ask for a more beautiful description of the action of Christ's Spirit? What more could one want from prayer?

Seventh Sunday of Easter

Bread and Wine

We all need heroes in this world. We need to remember the men and women who show us what baptism means, who nurture us, and who bring us into the ways of God. I've been thinking about such a person lately, a man named Horace McKenna, a Jesuit priest who spent his life working among the poor.

McKenna, said a co-worker, "didn't care where you came from or what ditch you got out of." He wasn't afraid to hold unpopular opinions or to endure trouble from religious superiors for the sake of the people. And all those who knew him agree that he never stopped giving and sacrificing for people broken by poverty, hunger, despair, or life itself.

This life was not easy for Horace McKenna. It was hard work, tiring work, and perhaps work he would rather not have done. "When God lets me into heaven," he said near the end of his life, "I think I'll ask to go off in a corner for half an hour and sit down and cry because the strain is off, the work is done, and I haven't been unfaithful or disloyal. All these needs that I have known are in the hands of Providence, and I don't have to worry any longer who's at the door, whose breadbox is empty, whose baby is sick, whose house is shaken and discouraged, and whose children can't read."

Horace was faithful to this work to the end, and when he died in 1982, a great crowd of the wealthy and the poor, blacks and whites gathered for his funeral. It was a great testimony to the life he lived. "In his own person," said the homilist, Horace "had broken down all lines, barriers, and distinctions between us. He is our reconciler, mediator, and peacemaker. He is the door through whom we pass to friendship with one another."

When I think of the eucharist, I tend to think of people like Horace. I think, too, of my parents who have sacrificed so much for the sake of my brother and sister and me. I think of the many married and single people I know who seem to bring a fundamental concern for others to everything they do.

When I think of the eucharist, I think of people who break down barriers and live as reconcilers and peacemakers. I think of people with responsibilities, families, and jobs who help us see that Christian discipleship isn't something to be squeezed into a busy life (and something that makes us feel guilty or inadequate because we can't do as much as someone else), but that it is, instead, the *fundamental force* of our busy lives, the how and why of everything we do.

And when I think of eucharist, I think, of course, of Christ. Christ taught us that life is to be lived for others or it isn't worth living. He proved this with his own dying and rising. He calls us into that same life through baptism and confirmation, and he strengthens us in that life with the gifts of bread and wine, gifts so rich that we will come to the end of time before we come to see the fullness of their meaning.

The eucharist comes to us out of many human and divine traditions of feeding, nurturing, sharing, and giving life for others. Food is the first gift a baby asks for and receives, and even our fast food culture, busy lives, and tendency to watch television during dinner have not totally destroyed what it means to gather for a meal. When we sit down at a meal together, we draw close to one another, share friendship, build solidarity, celebrate families and love, bring about reconciliation and healing, nourish relationships, thank and praise God, and receive sustenance for body and spirit. To sit down and eat with someone is still to share something special in that person's life. Even the much ridiculed and often hypocritical expression "Let's do lunch" still contains within it a faint echo of relationship, mutual interest, reconciliation, sought agreements, perhaps even covenant.

Scripture tells us that when God created the world, one of the first gifts to the man and woman was food. Scripture is full of references to God feeding God's people. The hospitality Abraham and Sarah show by preparing food and drink for the angels leads to God's promise to make them a great nation. The prophets and the psalmists sing of a heavenly banquet, and every year the Jews renew and deepen their covenant with God by gathering and sharing the meal of the passover.

Building on these meanings of sharing food and dining are the meals Jesus shares with his disciples, and the meal Jesus shares with us. The last supper is not the first or the last time we see Jesus blessing bread, breaking it, and giving it to the disciples and the people. For Jesus, breaking and sharing bread was very much a part of the covenant life he lived, a life of blessing and praising God, a life of feeding and nourishing, a life of breaking down barriers (for example, by eating with "sinners" and tax collectors), healing, reconciling, and giving of himself. Like the bread broken and the cup shared, Jesus himself was broken and poured out, consumed for the sake and life of the world.

Caught up within Christ's action, Christ's life of breaking, giving, offering, and sharing, are the bread and wine themselves. Bread was a basic staple of Christ's time (as it still is for many groups today). And the wine spoke of festivity and bounty.

But while both are common foods, given from the earth and the fruit of the vine, neither is a simple gift from God. Bread is not harvested ready-made from the earth the way carrots and potatoes are. And plucking a grape from a vine is not enough to give you wine. Human beings need to be more involved than that. Bread and wine come from the human work of cooperating with God and nature, the human work of harvesting the grain, crushing it, blending it, and making it a loaf, and picking the grapes, crushing them, blending them, and fermenting them into drink.

In the crushing and blending of grain and grapes lie powerful images of the church as the body of Christ, called to cooperate with Christ in the work of building the body, called to our very necessary share of his work. Because we are the body of Christ, we, too, are the bread and wine, called to be crushed and blended into one people, one loaf, one cup of wine with Christ, so that we too may be broken and poured out to bring nourishment to the world.

But like all our symbols, bread and wine speak about death as well as life. They too have their dark side, their shadow side, a side that can remind us of the aching hungers yet to be satisfied in our world.

Throughout our world food is used as a weapon, as an agent of discrimination. Unlike Jesus, we are usually very careful about whom we eat with. People go hungry while politicians and dictators of every persuasion jockey for advantage, and governments starve entire provinces in order to defeat rebel groups.

This shadow side is present in the midst of the assembly as well. There are persons who, because of remarriage after divorce, for example, aren't in full communion with the church. There are recovering alcoholics for whom drinking from the cup of wine may mean a return to a life of misery and addiction. There are persons with eating disorders who may not be able to think of our banquet the way the rest of us can. There are men and women burdened with serious doubts about God, the church, and the eucharist. There are those who feel so alone in this world that our joyous gathering for eucharist may serve (like Christmas or other holidays) only to reinforce their sense of loneliness. And in our assemblies, there are many couples united in mixed marriages who must separate at our most intense moment of communion—the Catholic spouse going alone to receive the bread and wine.

These are only a few examples. For many of us, in one way or another, our gathering and our meal of bread and wine can be signs of affliction and separation as well as of unity and life.

We live with this shadow side because we are not yet in heaven. Christ's victory over death is final, but not yet fully revealed. While we wait for that revelation we still live as broken people in a broken world. But God's promises are still alive, still active, still coming to us, even through signs that might appear broken because of who we are. Perhaps the gift of bread and wine is also a sign that God's grace works in this world through broken lives, a sign to remind us that not everyone gathers at this table yet, and a sign of how desperately we need to be real food, to help bring about the healing and reconciliation of the world in Christ.

When infants are baptized in the Eastern church today, they are also nourished with a drop of eucharistic wine. (In the early centuries the Western church followed this practice as well.) At the Easter Vigil, the newly baptized and anointed adults immediately join the assembly around the table for the feast of God's kingdom. When we gather for Mass this Sunday, as every Sunday, we assemble as one people to be nourished, to remember, to reaffirm, to move more deeply into the life of dying and rising and self-offering we began in baptism. We assemble as one body of Christ to pray and sing together, to tell our family stories together, to offer as one people our praise and thanks to God, and to speak of the goodness of both creation and the work of human hands. We ask the Spirit to come upon our gifts, and to fill us as well, so that we too may live more and more in Christ and share his mission.

And Christ in the power of the Spirit eats with us and nourishes us, so that we may return to the world stronger than we came in, more ready to follow in the footsteps of Horace McKenna and the other heroes and saints we know, more willing to offer ourselves for justice and reconciliation, more prepared to tear down barriers and be peacemakers, more able to be bread and wine for others, more able to be faithful to our covenant to the end.

Toward Pentecost Sunday

Acts 2:1–11
Psalm 104:1,24,29–30,31,34
1 Corinthians 12:3–7,12–13
John 20:19–23

MONDAY

We began our Easter journey on Ash Wednesday by hearing the prophet Joel tell us to rend our hearts not our garments, and to return to the Lord our God (Joel 2:13). We answered that call. In the past 14 weeks we have followed Christ into the grave and then rejoiced in his risen presence among us.

Now our special season of rejoicing is almost over. There is just one great feast left to celebrate—the day of Pentecost.

Just as we began our season of joy with the great Easter Vigil, so there is a Pentecost vigil to begin our final celebration of the season. And just as we began our paschal journey with the prophet Joel, so it is fitting that we return to him at this vigil (Joel 3:1–5) to hear the rest of the story, to hear God's promise to pour out the Spirit upon all of us and to "work wonders in the heavens and on the earth."

In the other readings of the vigil we see God confusing and scattering the people who were building their tower of Babel (Genesis 11:1–9). We see God making a covenant with our ancestors and coming down on Sinai in fire and smoke (Exodus 19:3–8,16–20). We hear God promise to take us from our graves and breathe the Spirit into our dry bones so that we might live (Ezekiel 37:1–14). We hear how God's Spirit intercedes for us as we wait in hope (Romans 8:22–27), and most important, we remember how the Spirit flows from baptism, from our share in the life of Jesus, whose death and resurrection give us the living water that rises within us (John 7:37–39).

As you pray over the readings of Pentecost day, keep these readings from the Pentecost vigil in mind as well. They can help us see that Pentecost is the story of what God has done in the past and is doing for us in our daily lives right now. They can help us see that Pentecost, like all of Easter, is about dying and rising, about baptism and covenant, about gifts and unity, about peace and justice, about reconciliation and hope, about fire and mission and life itself.

How has God spoken to you thus far in your Lent/Easter journey? What do you pray for as you approach Pentecost?

TUESDAY

First Reading: Acts 2:1–11
"All were filled with the Holy Spirit."

Long before the extraordinary event described here, Pentecost had been celebrated by the Jewish people. It was also known as their Feast of Weeks, and it occurred seven weeks and one day (Pentecost means 50 days) after the Feast of the Passover. It began as a festival of thanksgiving for the first fruits of the wheat harvest, and later became a day for commemorating God's covenant on Sinai as well. By the time of Jesus, Pentecost was a joyous feast for remembering the salvation of Israel.

Seven weeks after Christ's passover from death to life, Luke shows us the disciples gathered and praying on this day of Pentecost. And the same God who appears so often in the Hebrew Scriptures in the form of fire and wind and smoke rushes down from the heavens and fills the gathering with the Spirit. The community rises, as if from the grave, living now with God's strength, God's Spirit, and God's boldness. The members go out to a world of many nations, and the process of scattering and fragmenting that began with Babel is reversed. God begins to bring unity out of chaos. The good news is preached. And the baptisms that result from that preaching create the community of Christians we met on the Second Sunday of Easter, a community living in the Spirit and sharing all things in common. This is the Pentecost community of Christ's covenant, the first fruits of the harvest of redemption.

Revealing the truth of what happened on Pentecost is so important that Luke can only describe it in these scriptural images of the Jewish people. But the beauty and power of this language can also hide an important truth from us. It can tempt us to forget that this is *our* feast too and that the touch of God is meant to change our lives. It can tempt us to forget that we share in the gifts of the Spirit, that we are part of the people of the covenant, the first fruits of Christ's harvest, the community meant to be driven by the wind and fire of God's Spirit so that the harvest may be full and the salvation of our God may be remembered and shared by all.

What images of this reading speak to your life? How do you share in the gifts of the Spirit?

WEDNESDAY

Responsorial Psalm: Psalm 104:1,24,29–30,31,34
"When you send forth your spirit, they are created, and you renew the face of the earth."

The giving of the Spirit, a people renewed, a people on fire with the life of God—how could we keep from raising our voices in praise after hearing our first reading?

And since Pentecost began as an agricultural feast, what could be more appropriate than joining with Israel to praise God's work in nature, to sing of how God's spirit breathes forth life, creating, sustaining, and renewing the face of our earth?

But we have more to celebrate than that. For thousands of years this has been the feast of a covenant, and just as Luke builds his description of one Pentecost on images of the Hebrew Scriptures, so in this song we build upon their work as well and sing not just of God renewing our natural world, but of God's covenant promise to renew us by sending forth the Spirit that gives us breath and life, the Spirit that keeps us from being dried bones and dust.

But, again, we have even more to celebrate than that. Through Christ in the Spirit, we are a new creation and we have joined in the Spirit's work of building our world. So we sing of our hope that we may be sent out by the power of that Spirit to help create, sustain, and renew the face of the earth, both the natural world that is God's special gift to us, and all our brothers and sisters who fill that earth.

We sing of God's greatness for this work being done in us. And we pray that our God will be pleased with what we do, so that the glory of God may be seen, and felt, and endure forever.

Are you reluctant to sing this song of praise? How is God calling you to renew the face of the earth? How have you been renewed by the gift or touch of God's Spirit that has come to you from others?

THURSDAY

Second Reading: 1 Corinthians 12:3–7,12–13
"There are different gifts but the same Spirit."

The gift of the Spirit is a wonderful thing. It gives us new life and the power to renew our world. But we shouldn't take this wonderful gift for granted or feel triumphal about it, for, like water or fire or wind, the presence of the Spirit can bring destruction as well as joy. With the gift of the Spirit, as with all our resurrection stories, rising is never far removed from dying.

Just look at the Corinthians. In the opening greeting of his letter to them, Paul says that in Christ Jesus they have been "enriched in every way," and that they are "not lacking in any spiritual gift." And yet here is a community being torn apart by factions. The Corinthians had received so many gifts from God that they were literally being torn apart by their inability to cope with their diversity or power.

The same thing can happen today. Especially since Vatican II the church has been encouraging all the people to use and nurture the gifts the Spirit gives them. The more gifts we share, the greater our diversity and the greater our temptation to compare and compete and see our gifts as individual treasures. And soon it's the tower of Babel all over again.

So Paul's advice to the Corinthians is meant for us as well. The gifts of the Spirit are not individual treasures. They are meant for the common good. The first gift of the Spirit should be love and unity.

We should rejoice in our diversity and in all the ministries and gifts we have been given, for these may be signs of the strength of the Spirit in our lives. But Paul reminds us that we have our gifts only so that we may build up the entire body, so that Christ may build up and save the world.

We are only saved from Babel by remembering that we have all been given to drink of the one Spirit, that we must constantly seek the renewal of that Spirit in our communities, deepen our love of the risen Christ, and strengthen our baptismal connections to the one Body. That is the only way we may accomplish the work of the one God.

How do you put your gifts at the service of your community? How has your parish struggled to maintain unity in diversity?

FRIDAY

Gospel: John 20:19–23
"Peace be with you."

The gospel returns us to the community of disciples as we encountered them on the second Sunday of Easter. In their upper room, timid and discouraged, they are, like the dry bones Ezekiel spoke of, without hope or life.

But Jesus comes to them. He takes them out of their graves of fear. He breathes new life, new Spirit into them. And he leaves them with a mission.

But first he wishes them peace. Scripture scholars tell us that this greeting of "Peace be with you" is no ordinary greeting. It's the same language Jesus used to speak of the gift of the Spirit when he also said, "Do not let your hearts be troubled" (John 14:25–27). It is the same greeting of peace God used when Gideon came face to face with the angel of the Lord and thought he would die. God said to Gideon, "Peace be to you, do not fear, you shall not die" (Judges 6:23).

When we see the greeting in that light, I think it's also easier to see why Jesus showed the wounds of crucifixion still visible on his risen body. It's as if Christ is saying, "Peace be with you, do not fear, you shall not die, for through these wounds I have conquered death." Our redemption, our new life in the Spirit, and our peace all flow from these wounds, because Jesus suffered and sacrificed and lived for others. We should be calm and fearless, comforted, and full of hope and life because these wounds bring us into the presence of a loving, redeeming God, and God in the Spirit will stay with us.

This is the peace that Christ's Spirit breathes into us. This is why Christ was sent by the Father. This is the mission and the greeting he now asks us to bring to others—to spread the good news and the baptism that brings forgiveness of sins and eternal life. Christ calls us to be the signs of God's peace and reconciliation in the world, and to let that peace, that Spirit, that life, and that love flow from our own wounds, as they flowed from his. Christ calls us to be willing to suffer and sacrifice and live for one another, so that we may all know that we live in the presence of God.

How can you, your family, and your parish be signs of Christ's peace in the world?

SATURDAY

The Liturgical Prayers

Many of us speak of Pentecost as the birthday of the church.

This is when the Holy Spirit was given to the disciples and they began their mission.

But if this is true, what do we make of this Sunday's gospel? Didn't Jesus bring the Spirit to the disciples fifty days earlier, on the day of resurrection? Isn't it just as true to say that the church was born out of Christ's wounds on the cross on Good Friday? Did the Spirit come in a strong driving wind and tongues of fire on Pentecost, or in the gentle breath of Christ on Easter Sunday?

The scriptural answer to all these questions, of course, is yes. The Spirit came in all these ways and at all these times. God's Spirit has been active in the world since the beginning. The Spirit's gifts touched Abraham and Sarah, Moses, Ruth, Isaiah, all the prophets, and all the holy men and women of Israel.

With the death and resurrection of Christ, the fullness of that Spirit was given to our church throughout the ages—to the community of disciples, to the communities of the twelfth century when the Pentecost sequence was written, to the church of our fathers and mothers. And this same Spirit, sometimes coming in a driving wind and sometimes in a gentle, easily missed breath, has been given to us as well.

The Spirit is given lavishly to those who are open to its gifts. But many of us like to be spectators. We sit in our pews and listen to the stories of the disciples receiving the Spirit, as if they have nothing to do with us. Sometimes it seems safer that way, even if it isn't what Christ calls us to do.

But on this day of Pentecost, we pray together that we may be open to this Spirit, and that we—not others, *we*—may do the Spirit's work in the world. In the liturgical prayers of the day, and in the sequence, we pray that the Spirit will come upon us in driving winds and cooling graces and fill our lives. We stand before God in the light of Christ and pray to be drawn deeper into the Spirit, so that our lives, our church, and our world may be renewed.

Are you ready to ask God for the gift of the Spirit? Do you see the life of Christ as something you are called to be part of? How?

PENTECOST SUNDAY

It is the last of our fifty days. Our Great Sunday is coming to an end. We have lived joyfully in the presence of the risen Christ. We have seen and felt and tasted something that will be fully revealed only at the end of time. We have walked with Christ, and told our stories to one another, and perhaps, with the help of the Spirit, we've come to see a little more clearly what the risen Christ has done and is sending us out to do.

Now, after one last burst of joy, we get back to work. And we have our work cut out for us. We need to take all the lovely, powerful words of resurrection that we've spoken to one another, all the talk of God from Scripture and the liturgy, and start showing what they really mean by living them out in our daily lives.

Pick up your newspaper. Drive down your street. Look at your family. There is no end to the work Christ calls us to do. And the worst thing we can do, the greatest betrayal of our Lent/Easter season, is to look at a world crying out for Christ's healing and love, and do nothing.

All around us there are forces telling us we are insignificant and powerless, that we can do nothing to change the way things are. But Easter tells us something different. Easter tells us that the power of God lives in our world. Easter tells us that we, though still sinners, have received the lavish gifts of the Spirit so that we may join in God's work of renewing the earth. Easter gives us the strength to be living flames, to look beyond ourselves and our failings and our fears and to bring the healing touch of God's forgiveness, light, and joy to a world that knows too much of darkness, selfishness, and hatred.

It's daunting, discouraging work. We'll see a lot more of dying than of rising. But we have our faith, we have one another, we have the promise of the Spirit, and we have our Sunday gathering, the continuing weekly celebration of Easter. From all these sources the crucified and risen Christ breathes life into our dry bones, giving us strength and courage until that joyous day when we will all rise with him forever and live as children of the light.